Lecture Notes in Computer Science

Edited by G. Goos and J. Hartmanis

288

Andrzej Blikle

MetaSoft Primer

Towards a Metalanguage for
Applied Denotational Semantics

Springer-Verlag

Berlin Heidelberg New York London Paris Tokyo

Author

Andrzej Blikle
Institute of Computer Science
Polish Academy of Sciences
PKiN P.O. Box 22, 00-901 Warsaw, Poland

CR Subject Classification (1987): D.3.1, D.2.10, F.3.2−3

ISBN 3-540-18657-3 Springer-Verlag Berlin Heidelberg New York
ISBN 0-387-18657-3 Springer-Verlag New York Berlin Heidelberg

Printing and binding: Druckhaus Beltz, Hemsbach/Bergstr.
2145/3140-543210

FOREWORD

This book is devoted to a simplified version of denotational semantics, also known as *naive denotational semantics* (NDS), where sets are used in the place of Scott's reflexive domains and where jumps are described without continuations. The first public announcement of this approach dates back to [Blikle 82] and in a more complete version to [Blikle, Tarlecki 83]. Since then several experiments were undertaken in order to estimate the adequacy of NDS for applications. One group of experiments concerned the construction of models for typical software mechanisms such as procedures with parameters, blocks with local objects, jumps, escapes, exception handlers, pointers, user-defined types, error-handling mechanisms, concurrency. Another group was devoted to the construction of models for some typical software systems such as Pascal-like languages, Lisp-like languages, OCCAM^{TM}-like languages, word processors, operating systems or data-base management systems.

The mentioned experiments have proved that naive denotational semantics can be conveniently and rigorously used in applications. They also have led to the establishment of a kernel of a definitional metalanguage and of a general methodology of using denotational techniques in software design.

Our book is devoted to the former subject and consists of two parts. Part One starts from a general theory of chain-complete partially ordered sets (cpo's), continuous functions and their least fixed points. This theory provides a general mathematical framework for the recursive definitions of denotations, of their domains, of syntax and of the functions of semantics. Next we describe several calculi based on the cpo's of relations, functions, formal languages and domains, and we introduce a corresponding notation. Since the denotational definitions of software should serve not only the purpose of software specification, but also as a ground where one can prove the properties of software, we devote two sections to the introduction of appropriate logical tools. We introduce, and motivate, a calculus of three-valued predicates and then we discuss the derivation of Hoare's logic proof rules on that ground.

In Part two we show how to use the introduced mathematical tools in constructing a denotational definition of an existing programming language. We also show how to formulate and prove typical properties of the defined language and how to develop a corresponding program-correctness logic.

As a programming language in our example we have chosen Pascal. Since the size of the book does not permit to give a full definition of that language, we have restricted ourselves to its subset which contains basic commands and expressions and a (nearly) complete mechanism of arrays, records and pointers. On that ground we discuss the issue of user-definable types in programming languages and we show how to model them in NDS. We also point out how inadequate are the informal definitions of these mechanisms in the report of Pascal [Jensen, Wirth 78] and in the ISO standard of that language.

For the already mentioned sake of brevity we have excluded from our example both procedures and jumps — two software mechanisms which have stimulated the development of the so called *standard denotational semantics* (see Introduction). Readers interested in the description of these mechanisms within NDS, i.e. without the use of reflexive domains and continuations, should refer to [Blikle, Tarlecki 83]. We also omit methodological considerations which can be found in [Blikle 87]. It is argued there that in the process of software design one should develop denotations in the first place and then should derive syntax from them.

In the present form the notation introduced in Part One of our book can only be used in "handwritten" applications, i.e. without any specialized computer support. Although such applications also make sense — e.g. a formal definition of ADA (cf.[Bjørner,Oest 80]), which has later served in the development of ADA compiler in Dansk Datamatik Center, has been developed in that way — they require a sufficiently enthusiastic and well-trained team. Any broader use of denotational techniques in an industrial environment must be preceded by the development of a computer-support system consisting of a specialized editor, type checker, data-base facilities, rapid prototyping facilities and the like. This in turn requires the construction of a fully formalized definitional metalanguage with a sufficiently strong typing system, modularization techniques, proof support, etc. For the realization of that goal a five-year project **MetaSoft** has been initiated in Fall 1985 in the Institute of Computer Science of the Polish Academy of Science in Warsaw and Gdańsk. Part One of our book contains, therefore, the description of the semantic kernel of the future metalanguage of MetaSoft.

Our book is addressed to readers interested in the applications of denotational semantics: researchers who are developing projects similar to **MetaSoft**, software engineers interested in the formal methods of software specification, students of computer science departments. We hope that the book may also be used as a supplementary reading for university courses on applied denotational semantics and VDM. For that purpose a list of exercises has been included in Part One. The only prerequisites for the readers are the elementary set theory and logic, the elements of formal language theory and the ability of reading Pascal programs. A familiarity with standard denotational semantics, or with VDM, may help in appreciating our motivations but is not necessary.

At the end a few remarks about how to read this book. Since Part One introduces many mathematical constructions, not all of which are used in Part Two, readers interested primarily in applications may only glimpse through Part One in the first reading and return to it later. In that case in the first reading they may skip Sec.3, Sec.9 and Sec.10.

ACKNOWLEDGMENTS

My interest in applied denotational semantics started in Spring 1980
during a visit in Dines Bjørner's group at the Technical University
of Denmark in Lyngby. Discussions about VDM and its applications
inspired my research on a VDM-like denotational semantics. That work
was continued in May/March 1981 at the University of Linkoeping in
Sweden where I had the first opportunity of lecturing and discussing
a continuation-free denotational semantics [Blikle 81b]. The ideas
developed there and combined with a set-theoretic approach to domains
were presented in June 1982 at an IFIP's W.G.2.2 group meeting in
Garmisch-Partenkirchen. Andrzej Tarlecki contributed to them later
which resulted in a common paper [Blikle, Tarlecki 83] presented as
an invited lecture at the 1983 IFIP Congress in Paris.

The first draft of the present book was written in May 1983 during a
visit in the Istituto di Scienze dell'Informazione of the University
of Turin. Large parts of the material were discussed there in a
series of seminars. Andrea Maggiolo-Schettini contributed to an
(unpublished) exercise where a small database-management language was
defined in the NDS framework. The manuscript prepared in Turin was
revised and completed in August 1983 during my visit at the
Department of Computer Science of the University of Manchester.
Discussions with Cliff Jones and Derek Andrews substantially
contributed to both the theoretical part of the book and to the
example. This material was printed as [Blikle 83] in Pisa with the
support of CNR Projetto P_1 Cnet and was later used as class notes
for two of my courses: a course offered to a Special Interest Group
for Formal Methods of Software Engineering of the Polish Computer
Society in Warsaw in 1984, and another course given to students in
the Institute of Datalogy of the University of Copenhagen in Winter

1985. The listeners of both courses have communicated to me many relevant remarks. I also especially appreciated the discussions which I had with Niel Jones in Copenhagen.

The present version of Part One of the book was completed partly during my visit at the University of Pisa in September 1985 and partly in March/May 1986 when I was visiting again Dines Bjørner's group in Lyngby. Sec.9 on three-valued predicates was also discussed in seminars in Dansk Datamatik Center with the members of project **RAISE**.

To all the institutions mentioned above I wish to express my gratitude for excellent conditions and atmosphere which they have created for my work. Special thanks are also addressed to the listeners of my seminars and courses for many stimulating discussions and remarks.

Although the major part of the book has been written when I was working outside Poland, large parts of the material were thoroughly discussed with my Polish colleagues. Here special thanks should be addressed to Stefan Sokołowski and Andrzej Tarlecki, today both in the **MetaSoft** group, who have read and discussed with me some early versions of this book. Also Marek Lao, Marek Ryćko and Ida Szafrańska have communicated interesting remarks. No need to say that the responsibility for all mistakes which remain in the book is entirely of the author.

The list of acknowledgments would have been incomplete if I did not mention excellent books [Gordon 79] and [Stoy 77] which have introduced me into the realm of denotations. Last but certainly not least, the inspiring influence of Dana Scott's famous works on fixed points, domains and lambda-calculus models cannot be overestimated.

Warsaw in August 1987   Andrzej Blikle

INTRODUCTION

The method of denotational semantics has been developed at the beginning of the decade 1970-80 as a mathematical technique of writing implementation- -independent definitions of software. Conceptually it has its roots in mathematical logic, where the meaning of an expression is a function and the meaning of a whole is a combination of the meanings of its parts. Technically, however, it has to deal with much more complicated mechanisms.

The pioneers of denotational semantics have felt particularly challenged by the problem of describing the mathematically most unnatural features of ALGOL-60: the self-applicability of procedures (a procedure may take itself as a parameter) and jumps nested in structured programs. The former problem has led to a model of **reflexive domains** [Scott 71] and [Scott 76], the latter to a technique of **continuations** [Strachey, Wadsworth 1974]. Their combination gave a powerful definitional method known today as **standard denotational semantics** (SDS). A full definition of ALGOL-60 in the SDS style was given in [Mosses 74].

Standard denotational semantics quickly became known and appreciated in the academic community. Its most important contribution to the formal specification of software consists in providing the first mathematical model for a compositional (i.e. inductively defined) semantics of complex programming languages and in stimulating broad research aimed at the applications of mathematics in software design.

Unfortunately the applications of (pure) SDS have remained rather limited. Although SDS formally provides an adequate ground where to define (old) and design (new) software, none of widely used programming languages has been designed in using SDS and only very few have been given SDS definitions later.

The discrepancy between the potential advantages of SDS and its actual applications has not been caused by the lack of interest of software engineers in formal methods. The main obstacles of broader applications of SDS have always been of a rather technical nature:
- the lack of a convenient notation (metalanguage) for real-life applications,
- the conceptual and technical complexity of reflexive domains and continuations.

The first major breakthrough in this situation was offered by Vienna Development Method (VDM) [Bjørner, Jones 78]. That method has provided a metalanguage, called META-IV, suitable for large denotational definitions and offering a technique of defining jumps without continuations [Jones 78]. The authors of VDM also decided to treat the Scott model of reflexive domains informally by assuming that for a practical purpose reflexive domains may be "regarded" as sets. At that point they were later supported by other authors who popularized denotational semantics, such as M.Gordon [Gordon 79] or J.Stoy [Stoy 80].

The philosophy and techniques of VDM proved to be useful in many applications. Formal definitions of PL/1, ALGOL-60, Standard Pascal, Pascal R, Pascal Plus, Modula-2, Edison, CHILL, Prolog and Ada have been written in the VDM style (see [Bjørner, Phren 83] for references). This resulted in a better understanding of these systems and in finding many ambiguities and inconsistencies in them. Some of these definitions, e.g. of Pascal Plus, Edison, CHILL and Ada, have been used later in the development of compilers. Several data-base systems (or their parts) were formally defined, e.g. the PL/1 programmers' interface to full concurrent System/R, System 2000 and CODASYL/DBTG. Some aspects of operating systems, office automation systems and the like have been defined in VDM style and were partly used later in implementations. All these examples have convinced many practitioners that denotational semantics may be a handy tool in real-life applications. Many universities started to offer regular courses on VDM. Some industrial institutions decided to consider VDM as their standard for software specification.

The vulgarization of Scott's model in VDM has very well paid in the applications where a formal definition of software is used only as a formalized reference-manual for human readers. It seems, however, questionable whether such a vulgarization can provide an adequate framework for proving the correctness of software or for the development of systems that support code generation. Besides, it is rather inconsistent to proclaim and advocate mathematical style and at the same time to agree for the violation of mathematical rules at the most critical point of the model. This may also lead to technical inconsistencies since reflexive domains and sets behave differently (form essentially different algebras), especially if fixed-point equations are concerned. Moreover, some domain constructors used in VDM, such as e.g. $A - B$, $A \overset{3}{\rightarrow} B$ or $A \underset{m}{\rightarrow} B$ are not definable for reflexive domains.

The theoreticians of VDM (cf.[Stoy 80]) suggest several technical remedies to these problems. In order to make the algebra of reflexive domains closer to the algebra of sets, some operations, like products, must be redesigned and some others, like subtraction, must be forbidden. One also has to forget about the difference between partial functions, total functions and mappings and represent all of them by continuous functions between cpo's.

All these technical restrictions are not very convenient in applications and therefore are not very rigidly observed by VDM users. For instance, one frequently relies on the fact that mappings are finite-domain functions and therefore a test whether an element belongs to the domain of a mapping is computable.

The discrepancy between the theory and practice of VDM puts a formal question-mark on the consistency of VDM definitions. On the other hand, when reading such definitions one usually has a strong impression that they are not inconsistent. In fact these definitions can most frequently be given consistent interpretations since in the majority of software systems one does not deal with self-applicability and therefore all semantic domains may be regarded as sets. This is obviously true for most operating systems, communication protocols, data-base management systems, spread-sheets, word processors, etc. This is also true for nearly all modern programming languages including Pascal, Modula, Ada, OCCAM and many others.

Self-applicability in programming languages appears essentially in only two standard situations:

1) if procedural recursion is elaborated dynamically, like in Lisp;

2) if a procedure may be directly or indirectly passed to itself as an actual parameter, like in Algol—60.

A glance on programming languages which were designed after 1970 shows a clear tendency to avoiding both these mechanisms. Static binding has been considered safer than dynamic binding and procedures are usually restricted in a way which protects them against self-applicability. For all such languages semantic domains may be just sets.

As was already mentioned in the Foreword, in this book we describe a kernel of a metalanguage for a set-theory based denotational semantics. We define and discuss several mathematical tools which are useful in constructing the denotational models of software in that style. The notation which we propose has been strongly influenced by META-IV. However, in contrast to the former, our metalanguage is going to be a pure functional language. The major extensions with respect to META-IV are binary relations, languages with infinite words, McCarthy's three-valued predicates and program—correctness statements.

C O N T E N T S

P A R T   O N E

DENOTATIONAL CONSTRUCTORS

Sec.1

INTRODUCTION

Every denotational model of a software system is described in terms of some sets, functions and relations. In this part of the book we define basic constructors of such objects and we introduce an appropriate notation.

In Sec.2 we briefly introduce the theory of fixed points in partially ordered sets. This is a traditional framework used in denotational semantics for recursive definitions. In Sec.3 we define a calculus of binary relations which serves later as a common ground for the construction of several calculi used in the description of input-output models of software. On that ground we develop later a calculus of functions (Sec.4 and Sec.5) and we show how to tackle the problem of input-output correctness at a model-theoretic ground (Sec.10). Sec.6 is devoted to tuples and Cartesian products. This prepares a ground for the introduction of a calculus of formal languages (Sec.7). In Sec.8 we introduce a calculus of domains. Sec.9 is devoted to a calculus of three-valued predicates. We use that calculus — in the place of classical two-valued calculus — in the mathematical models of software, in formulating the properties of software and in software correctness proof rules. The latter are discussed in Sec.10.

FIXED—POINT EQUATIONS AND THE THEORY OF CPO'S

Let us start from fixing some basic notation for sets and functions which we shall use throughout this book. If A and B denote sets, then A|B, A∩B, AxB and A—B denote the union, the intersection, the Cartesian product, and the difference of A and B respectively. If **A** denotes a family of sets, then U**A** and ∩**A** denote the union and the intersection of all the elements of **A**. φ denotes the empty set. If f:A→B is a function from A to B and a∈A, then by f.a we denote f(a). This is known as a **dot notation** and has been introduced for the sake of dealing with so called **curried functions** (Sec.5). In this notation every function is regarded as a one—argument function, where an argument may be a tuple. E.g. if g:AxB→C, then each argument of g is of the form ⟨a,b⟩ and therefore g.⟨a,b⟩ denotes the value of g in ⟨a,b⟩.

An equation of the form

$$x = f.x \tag{2.1}$$

where f:A→A is a total function from a set A into A is called a **fixed—point equation**. Any solution of such an equation is called a **fixed point** of f. Fixed—point equations provide a definitional technique which generalizes recursive definitions and which is frequently used in denotational semantics. A typical example of a fixed—point definition may be the following BNF—style grammar of a set (language) of Boolean expressions Exp:

$$Exp = Ide \mid \{not\}^\wedge Exp \mid \{(\}^\wedge Exp^\wedge \{or\}^\wedge Exp^\wedge \{)\} \mid \tag{2.2}$$
$$\{(\}^\wedge Exp^\wedge \{and\}^\wedge Exp^\wedge \{)\}$$

where Ide denotes some predefined set of identifiers and "^" denotes the concatenation of formal languages. This definition has the form of a fixed—point equation:

Exp = f.Exp

where f is the following function on languages:

f.L = Ide | {**not**}^L | {(}^L^{**or**}^L^{)} | {(}^L^{**and**}^L^{)}

A fixed-point equation may have no solution, exactly one solution or more than one solution. If therefore, we intend to regard an equation of the form (2.1) as a definition of x, then we must prove the existence and the uniqueness of its solution. Below we briefly describe a general theory where one can carry out such proofs.

By a **partially ordered set**, in short a **poset**, we mean an ordered pair (D,⊑) where D is an arbitrary nonempty set and where ⊑ ⊆ D×D is a binary relation such that for any a,b,c∈D the following conditions are satisfied:

1) a ⊑ a   reflexivity
2) a ⊑ b **and** b ⊑ c **implies** a ⊑ c   transitivity
3) a ⊑ b **and** b ⊑ a **implies** a = b   weak antisymmetry

The formula a ⊑ b is read "a is **smaller** than b", or "a **approximates** b. The relation ⊑ is called a **partial order** in D. A typical example of a poset is any family (set) of sets partially ordered by the set-theoretic inclusion.

For any A⊆D an element a∈A is called the least element of A, if it is smaller than any element of A, i.e. if a⊑a′ holds for any a′∈A. A set may have no least element, but if it has one, then this element must be unique. Indeed, if a and b are both the least elements of A, then a⊑b and b⊑a, hence by 3) a=b.

An element a∈A is called a **minimal** **element** of A if there is no element of A which is smaller than a, i.e. if there is no a′∈A such that a′⊑ a. A set may have no minimal element, one minimal element or more than one minimal element. A minimal element need not to be the least element, but the least element is always a (unique) minimal element. For instance, in the family of sets:

A = {{a,b,c},{a,b},{b,c}}

there are two minimal elements {a,b} and {b,c} but no least element. If, however, we add to A the set {b}, then {b} becomes the unique minimal element and the least element at the same time.

For any $A \subseteq D$ an element $d \varepsilon D$ is called an **upper bound** of A if it is greater than any element of A, i.e. if $a \sqsubseteq d$ for any $a \varepsilon A$. If the set of all upper bounds of A is not empty and contains the least element, then this element is called the **least upper bound** (abbreviated **lub**) of A and is denoted by $\sqcup A$. If A contains only two elements, i.e. if $A=\{a,b\}$, then we write $a \sqcup b$ instead of $\sqcup\{a,b\}$. As is easy to show, "$\sqcup$" is associative, hence we can write $a_1 \sqcup a_2 \sqcup \cdots \sqcup a_n$.

By a **chain** in D we mean a sequence of successively greater elements:

$$a_1 \sqsubseteq a_2 \sqsubseteq \cdots$$

By the **limit of a chain** we mean the least upper bound of all its elements. We denote this lub by $\sqcup_{i=1}^{\infty} a_i$. Of course, not every chain has a limit. For instance, in the poset of all finite sets of integers ordered by inclusion, the chain

$$\{1\} \subseteq \{1,2\} \subseteq \{1,2,3\} \subseteq \cdots$$

has no limit.

A poset $(D, \sqsubseteq)$ is called a **chain—complete partially ordered set**, in short a **cpo**, if every chain in D has a limit and if D has the least element. This least element is called the **bottom** of D and in the abstract case is denoted by $\perp$.

In our applications we use only a few basic types (classes) of cpo's plus cpo's which may be constructed from the basic ones by a few standard operations. A detailed discussion of all cpo's which are of interest for us is given in the sections which follow. Below we give only a few typical examples.

A cpo of subsets. If A—set denotes the family of all subsets of A, then (A—set, $\subseteq$) is a cpo with the empty set ϕ as the least element.

A cpo of partial functions. If $A \tilde{+} B$ denotes the set of all partial functions from A to B, then $(A \tilde{+} B, \sqsubseteq)$ is a cpo with the empty function ϕ as the least element. The ordering of functions by inclusion (functions are sets of pairs hence can be ordered by inclusion) is called the **horizontal ordering** of functions.

A cpo is called a **set—theoretic cpo** if:

1) all its elements are sets,
2) the corresponding partial order is the set—theoretic inclusion,
3) the limits of the chains (of sets) are the unions of sets.

Both cpo's described above are, of course, set—theoretic ones. As is easy to show there exist cpo's which satisfy 1) and 2), but which do not satisfy 3). As an example take the cpo of all finite sets of positive integers plus the set of all integers.

A flat cpo. Over any set A we can construct a (slightly artificial) cpo by adding to A an element $\perp$ and establishing in $A|\{\perp\}$ the following ordering:

$a \sqsubseteq b$ iff $a = \perp$ or $a = b$.

In a flat cpo all elements of A are mutually incomparable and $\perp$ is smaller than any of them. That situation is illustrated on Fig.2.1. Arrows indicate the ordering.

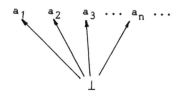

Fig.2.1

As was mentioned above, cpo's may be constructed from other cpo's by means of some standard operations. Below we define three major such operations:

The Cartesian product of cpo's. Given two cpo's $(A, \sqsubseteq_A)$ and

$(B, \sqsubseteq_B)$ their Cartesian product is a cpo $(A \times B, \sqsubseteq)$ where

$$(a_1, b_1) \sqsubseteq (a_2, b_2) \quad \text{iff} \quad a_1 \sqsubseteq_A a_2 \text{ and } b_1 \sqsubseteq_B b_2$$

The ordering of that cpo is called a **componentwise ordering**. This construction may be generalized to an arbitrary finite or infinite number of component cpo's.

The cpo of total functions. Let A be an arbitrary set and let $(B, \sqsubseteq_B)$ be an arbitrary cpo. The cpo of total functions $(A \rightarrow B, \sqsubseteq)$ is ordered by:

$$f \sqsubseteq g \quad \text{iff} \quad f.a \sqsubseteq_B g.a \quad \text{for any} \quad a \varepsilon A.$$

This is called an **argumentwise ordering** or a **vertical ordering** of total functions. If by analogy to the Cartesian plane we regard B as the (vertical) axis of values, then $f \sqsubseteq g$ means that every value of g is "above" the value of f for the same argument. In other words, the graph of g is above the graph of f. Observe that in the horizontal ordering defined earlier $f \sqsubseteq g$ means that the graph of f is contained in the graph of g. Observe that total functions ordered horizontally do not constitute a cpo since in that ordering they are all incomparable and therefore do not contain the least element. In $(A \rightarrow B, \sqsubseteq)$ the least element is a constant function which for all arguments assumes the value $\perp_B$.

The disjoint union of cpo's. Let $(A, \sqsubseteq_A)$ and $(B, \sqsubseteq_B)$ be two cpo's. If $A \cap B = \phi$, then the union of our cpo's is $(A_1 | B_1 | \{\perp\}, \sqsubseteq)$ where:

$$A_1 = A - \{\perp_A\},$$
$$B_1 = B - \{\perp_B\},$$
$$\perp \notin A_1 | B_1$$

and where the ordering is defined as follows:

$$a \sqsubseteq b \quad \text{iff} \quad \text{either} \quad a = \perp$$
$$\text{or} \quad a, b \; \varepsilon \; A_1 \text{ and } a \sqsubseteq_A b$$
$$\text{or} \quad a, b \; \varepsilon \; B_1 \text{ and } a \sqsubseteq_B b$$

In other words, we glue the least elements of A and B together, leave the orderings within A and B unchanged and assume that the elements of A are incomparable with the elements of B (Fig.2.2)

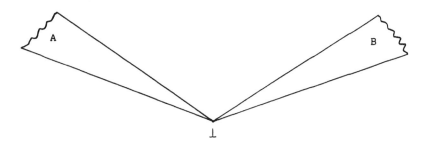

Fig.2.2

If A and B are not disjoint, then we have to separate them before making a union, e.g. by replacing A by $\{1\} \times A$ and B by $\{2\} \times B$. Similarly to Cartesian products also the union of cpo's may be defined for an arbitrary finite or infinite number of components.

On the ground of cpo's one can identify functions whose fixed points exist and are unique. We discuss such functions below.

Let $(A, \sqsubseteq_A)$ and $(B, \sqsubseteq_B)$ be two arbitrary cpo's and let $f : A \rightarrow B$. We say that f is **monotone** if it transfers the order of A into the order of B i.e. if

$$a_1 \sqsubseteq_A a_2 \quad \textbf{implies} \quad f.a_1 \sqsubseteq_B f.a_2$$

We say that f is **continuous** if it transfers chains and their limits from A into B, i.e. if for any chain

$$a_1 \sqsubseteq_A a_2 \sqsubseteq_A \ldots$$

its image by f is also a chain, i.e.

$$f.a_1 \sqsubseteq_B f.a_2 \sqsubseteq_B \ldots$$

and if

$$f.(\bigsqcup_{i=1}^{\infty} a_i) = \bigsqcup_{i=1}^{\infty} f.a_i$$

As is easy to show, any continuous function is monotone. The converse implication is not true. To see that consider the following example. Let Nat denote the set of all natural numbers, let Sub = {A|A Nat} be the cpo of all subsets of Nat ordered by inclusion and let f:Sub→Sub where:

$$f.A = A \quad \text{for finite A,}$$
$$\text{Nat} \quad \text{for infinite A}$$

This function is, of course, monotone but is not continuous since e.g. U{{2},{2,4},{2,4,6},...} = Even, where Even denotes the set of all even numbers, whereas

$$f.U\{\{2\},\{2,4\},\{2,4,6\},...\} = f.\text{Even} = \text{Nat}$$
$$U\{f.\{2\},f.\{2,4\},f.\{2,4,6\},...\} = \text{Even}$$

Other examples of monotone but not continuous functions are the domain constructors such as e.g. A—set, $A^{c\omega}$ or A⅁B which we define in Sec.8.

The property of continuity has a very natural motivation on the ground of computability theory. Consider an element aεA and assume that it cannot be represented in a computer, but that it can be approximated by representable elements. In other words, assume that $a = \bigsqcup_{i=1}^{\infty} a_i$ and that each a_i is representable. For instance, a may be a function defined for all integers and each a_i may denote its finite approximation (a partial function) defined for the first i arguments. Assume further that we wish to compute f.a for some f. Since a is not representable we cannot perform that task directly. The best we can do is to take a sufficiently good approximation a_i of a, to compute $f.a_i$ and to hope that $f.a_i$ will sufficiently well approximate the value of f.a. The continuity of f guaranties that such a hope is justified.

For our applications we are interested in continuous functions mainly because of the following property of their fixed points.

Let f:A→A and let (A,⊑) be a cpo. If the set of all fixed points of f is not empty and contains the least element, then this element is called the least fixed point (abbreviated lfp) of f and is denoted by Y.f. Of course, the least fixed point of f, if it exists, is unique.

Theorem 2.1 [Kleene 52] If $f:A \to A$ is continuous, then the least fixed point Y.f of f exists and

$$Y.f = \bigsqcup_{i=1}^{\infty} f^i \cdot \bot$$

where $f^1 \cdot \bot = f \cdot \bot$ and $f^{i+1} \cdot \bot = f \cdot (f^i \cdot \bot)$.

Proof. First we prove that $\{f^i \cdot \bot\}_{i=1}^{\infty}$ is a chain. Observe that $\bot \sqsubseteq f \cdot \bot$, since $\bot$ is the least element of A. Now by the monotonicity of f we prove by induction $f^i \cdot \bot \sqsubseteq f^{i+1} \cdot \bot$ for $i=1,2,\ldots$. Since $\{f^i \cdot \bot\}_{i=1}^{\infty}$ is a chain, its lub exists and since f is continuous we have

$$f \cdot (\bigsqcup_{i=1}^{\infty} f^i \cdot \bot) = \bigsqcup_{i=1}^{\infty} f^{i+1} \cdot \bot$$
$$= \bigsqcup_{i=1}^{\infty} f^i \cdot \bot$$

Therefore $\bigsqcup_{i=1}^{\infty} f^i \cdot \bot$ is a fixed point of f. In order to show that it is a lfp of f take an arbitrary fixed point a of f. Since $\bot \sqsubseteq a$, we prove by the monotonicity of f that $f^i \cdot \bot \sqsubseteq f^i \cdot a = a$. Hence $\bigsqcup_{i=1}^{\infty} f^i \cdot \bot \sqsubseteq a$. []

Below we quote a few simple theorems which are useful in proving the continuity of functions. Easy proofs of these theorems are left to the Reader.

Theorem 2.2 Every constant function is continuous.

Theorem 2.3 If A is a flat cpo and B is an arbitrary cpo, then every monotone function $f:A \to B$ is continuous.

Functions $f:A \to B$ with the property $f \cdot \bot_A = \bot_B$ are called strict. As is easy to see, if both A and B are flat, then if f is strict, then f is monotone (but not vice versa), hence also continuous. This implies further that every partial function $f:A \to B$ where A and B are ordinary sets (i.e. not cpo's) may be extended to a continuous function $f':A_\bot \to B_\bot$ where $A_\bot = A | \{\bot_A\}$ and $B_\bot = B | \{\bot_B\}$ are flat cpo's and where

$$f' \cdot a = \begin{cases} f \cdot a & \text{if } f \cdot a \text{ is defined} \\ \bot_B & \text{if } f \cdot a \text{ is undefined} \\ \bot_B & \text{if } a = \bot_A \end{cases}$$

Simplifying a little we may say that any function between sets may be regarded as a continuous function between the corresponding flat cpo's.

Complex continuous functions are usually constructed from simpler ones in using some continuity-preserving operations on functions. Below we define three typical such operations.

The composition of functions. If $f:A \to B$ and $g:B \to C$, then $f \cdot g:A \to C$ where $(f \cdot g).a = g.(f.a)$.

The conditional union of functions. Let Bool denote a flat cpo over $\{tt, ff\}$ with $\perp_B$. If $p:A \to Bool$ and $f,g:A \to C$, then

$$\text{IF } p \text{ THEN } f \text{ ELSE } g \text{ FI} : A \to C \quad \text{where,}$$

$$(\text{IF } p \text{ THEN } f \text{ ELSE } g \text{ FI}).a = \begin{cases} f.a & \text{if} \quad p.a = tt, \\ g.a & \text{if} \quad p.a = ff \\ \perp_C & \text{if} \quad p.a = \perp_B \end{cases}$$

The Cartesian product of functions. If $f:A \to B$ and $g:A \to C$, then $f \times g:A \to B \times C$ where $(f \times g).a = (f.a, g.a)$.

Observe that all three operations are in fact schemes of operations parameterized by A, B and C.

Theorem 2.4 The operations of composition, conditional union and Cartesian product preserve the continuity of their arguments.

If $A_1, \ldots, A_n$ are cpo's, then also $A_1 \times \ldots \times A_n$ is a cpo and therefore we can talk about the continuity of $f:A_1 \times \ldots \times A_n \to B$.

Theorem 2.5 $f:A_1 \times \ldots \times A_n \to B$ is continuous iff for every $i \leq n$ and any $a_j \varepsilon A$ with $j \neq i$ the one-argument function

$$f.\langle a_1, \ldots, a_{i-1}, x, a_{i+1}, \ldots, a_n \rangle$$

is continuous.

Now consider two arbitrary cpo's A and B and the corresponding cpo of total functions $(A \to B, \sqsubseteq)$. It is not difficult to show that the limit of a chain of continuous functions in $A \to B$ is a continuous function. Since the constant function, which is the bottom of $(A \to B, \sqsubseteq)$ is obviously a continuous function, we have the following theorem:

Theorem 2.6 For any cpo's A and B the set of all continuous function from A into B constitutes a cpo with vertical ordering.

As a simple corollary of that theorem we may observe that if a function $F: (A \to B) \to (A \to B)$ preserves continuity and is continuous itself, then its lfp Y.F is a continuous function from A into B.

BINARY RELATIONS

As was mentioned earlier, the calculus of binary relations constitutes a general mathematical framework where other calculi used in the mathematical modeling of software may be derived. Since we shall define our calculus on a set-theoretic ground we start this section from a recollection of the notation which we use for sets.

If A and B denote sets, then A|B, AnB, A×B and A—B denote the union, the intersection, the Cartesian product and the difference of sets. By UA and ∩A we denote respectively the union and the intersection of the family of sets. By φ we denote the empty set.

For any sets A and B any subset of their Cartesian product

$$R \subseteq A \times B$$

is called a **binary relation** between A and B. By

$$Rel.\langle A,B \rangle = \{R \mid R \subseteq A \times B\}$$

we denote the set of all binary relations between A and B. The fact that $\langle a,b \rangle \varepsilon R$ is also written as R(a,b), or aRb. The elements a and b are referred to as the **left argument** and the **right argument** or as the **input** and the **output** of R respectively.

Since relations are sets, all set-theoretic operations apply to relations. In particular φ denotes an empty relation. Whenever this leads to no confusion, binary relations are simply called **relations**.

Besides the mentioned set-theoretic operations we define a so called **sequential composition** of relations. For any two relations $R\varepsilon Rel.\langle A,B \rangle$ and $P\varepsilon Rel.\langle C,D \rangle$ we define:

$R \cdot P = \{\langle a,d\rangle \mid (\exists x \varepsilon B \cap C)(aRx \textbf{ and } xPd)\}$

Of course, if $B \cap C = \phi$, then $R \cdot P = \phi$. In particular $R \cdot \phi = \phi$ and $\phi \cdot R = \phi$ for any relation R. We say that ϕ is a **zero** of the operation "$\cdot$".

In all cases where this leads to no confusion we omit the symbol "$\cdot$" and write RP rather than $R \cdot P$. We also assume that composition binds stronger than union, i.e. that PQ | R means (PQ) | R.

The operation of composition has two important properties. It is **associative**, i.e.

$P(RQ) = (PR)Q$

and is **distributive** over unions, i.e.

$P(R|Q) = PR \mid PQ$ and
$(R|Q)P = RP \mid QP$

The distributivity holds for arbitrary finite and infinite unions and implies the following property of **monotonicity**:

if $P \subseteq R$ then $PQ \subseteq RQ$ and $QP \subseteq QR$.

The laws of the calculus of relations may be intuitively explained on the ground of nondeterministic networks of input—output modules. If we assume, that every relation R ε Rel.$\langle A,B\rangle$ represents a (possibly nondeterministic) module with inputs from A and outputs from B denoted by:

then R|P and RP represent respectively the networks:

Now, the associativity of composition allows us to construct chain networks of the form:

and distributivity guaranties the input-output equivalence of the following networks:

and

The same is, of course, true for the right-hand-side distributivity.

By analogy to the composition of two relations we define the composition of a relation and a set. If $R \varepsilon Rel.\langle A, B \rangle$ and C is a set, then CR and RC are sets defined as follows:

$$CR = \{b \mid (\exists c)(c \varepsilon C \text{ and } cRb)\}$$
$$RC = \{a \mid (\exists c)(aRc \text{ and } c \varepsilon C)\}$$

The set CR is called the **image** of C through R and contains all the "outputs" generated by R from the "inputs" which belong to C. The set RC is called the **coimage** of C through R and contains all the "inputs" of R which may generate "outputs" in C. The sets

$$rng.R = AR \quad \text{and}$$
$$dom.R = RB$$

are called the **range** and the **domain** of R respectively.

The composition of relations with sets has a restricted associativity property, i.e.

$$C(RP) = (CR)P \quad \text{and}$$
$$(RP)C = R(PC)$$

but in general

$$R(CP) \neq (RC)P$$

To see that take $R = \{\langle a,b \rangle\}$, $C = \{c\}$ and $P = \{\langle c,b \rangle\}$.

The distributivity over arbitrary unions — hence also the monotonicity — of that operation with respect to both relations and sets also holds.

If we extend the network model of relations to sets by assuming that sets may be interpreted alternatively as generators or as acceptors:

$$\boxed{C}\!\!> \text{-->} \qquad or \qquad \text{-->}\!\!<\boxed{C}$$

then CR and RC may be interpreted respectively as

$$\boxed{C}\!\!>\text{-->}\boxed{R}\!\!>\text{-->} \qquad and \qquad \text{-->}\!\!<\boxed{R}\!\!>\text{-->}\!\!<\boxed{C}$$

Again, the associativity and the distributivity properties may be illustrated in that model analogously as in the former case.

As the second pure relational operation we define the **inverse** of a relation:

$$R^{-1} = \{<b,a> \mid aRb\}$$

This operation is monotone wrt inclusion, distributive over unions and has a reverse distributivity property over composition, i.e.:

$$R \subseteq P \quad \textbf{implies} \quad R^{-1} \subseteq P^{-1},$$
$$(R|P)^{-1} = R^{-1}|P^{-1}$$
$$(RP)^{-1} = P^{-1}R^{-1}$$

Another important concept is an **identity relation** in a set. For any set A we denote:

$$id.A = \{<a,a> \mid a\varepsilon A\}$$

Of course, every identity relation is a function. In our network model id.A may be interpreted as a (deterministic) module which tests whether the arriving data belongs to A (satisfies a given condition) and if this is the case, then it passes this data unchanged, otherwise it aborts.

The composition of an identity relation id.C with a relation R results in the restriction of the domain or the range of R

depending whether   id.C   comes as the left- or the right-hand-side
argument of the composition:

$$(id.C)R = \{\langle a,b \rangle \mid a \varepsilon C \text{ and } aRb\}$$
$$R(id.C) = \{\langle a,b \rangle \mid aRb \text{ and } b \varepsilon C\}$$

Using the introduced operations we can define several properties of
relations such as reflexivity, symmetricity, functionality, etc.
Below we give a few more important examples of such definitions. Let
$R \ \varepsilon$ Rel.$\langle A,B \rangle$:

1) id.A $\subseteq$ R	R is **reflexive**,
2) $R \subseteq R^{-1}$	R is **symmetric**,
3) $RnR^{-1} \subseteq$ id.A	R is **weakly antisymmetric**,
4) RR $\subseteq$ R	R is **transitive**,
5) $R^{-1}R \subseteq$ id.B	R is a **function** from A to B,
6) 5) **and** $RR^{-1} \subseteq$ id.A	R is a **1-1 function** from A to B,
7) 5) **and** A = RB	R is a **total function** from A to B,
8) 5) **and** B = AR	R is a **onto-function** from A to B.

Our calculus of relations, and especially its particular instance —
the calculus of functions (see Sec. 4) — will be frequently used in
this book in the construction of complex relations and functions.
Since such constructions may involve fixed-point techniques, it is
necessary to establish a cpo of relations. The cpo which we are going
to use is (Rel.$\langle A,B \rangle$, $\subseteq$), where $\subseteq$ denotes the set-theoretic
inclusion of relations. The least element of that cpo is, of course,
the empty relation ϕ. As is easy to check the operations of union,
composition and reverse are continuous in this cpo.

Now let us consider a special case of Rel.$\langle A,B \rangle$ where A=B. That case
appears very frequently in our applications. Typically   A is a set
of states of some abstract machine and the elements of Rel.$\langle A,A \rangle$
represent state-transition relations. If our machine is
deterministic, then these relations are functions. In Rel.$\langle A,A \rangle$ we
define four following operations:

1) R^{r0}	= id.A		zero power,
2) R^{rn}	= RR^{rn-1}	for n > 0	n-th power,
3) R^{r+}	= $U_{n=1}^{\infty} R^{rn}$		plus iteration,
4) R^{r*}	= $U_{n=0}^{\infty} R^{rn}$		star iteration.

All these operations are continuous in (Rel.<A,A>, $\subseteq$).

In the sequel we shall frequently omit the discriminator "r" and write e.g. R^* rather than R^{r*}. We have introduced this discriminator in order to distinguish between operations on relations and similarly denoted operations on languages and on sets (cf. Sec.7 and Sec.8). In this book we shall use "r" only where its omission may lead to confusion. Of course, at the level of a formalized metalanguage (cf. our remarks in the Foreword) we have to use "r" permanently.

The star iteration is most frequently used to express the behavior of loops. E.g. the input—output relation of a **while**-loop command **while** a∈B **do** R **od** which corresponds to the diagram:

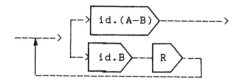

is $[(id.B)R]^* id.(A-B)$. It is also easy to prove, using Kleene's theorem (see Sec.2), that this relation is the least solution of the following equation:

$$X = id.(A-B) \mid (id.B)RX$$

In the same way one can prove that R^* and R^+ are the least solutions of $X = id.A \mid RX$ and of $X = R \mid RX$ respectively and describe the behavior of the following loops:

$$R^+ :: \qquad \text{and} \qquad R^* ::$$

The last concept which we discuss in this section is an equivalence relation. We say that R∈Rel.<A,A> is an **equivalence relation** in A if for any a,b,c which belong to A:

a R a

a R b **implies** b R a

a R b **and** b R c **implies** a R c.

i.e. if R is reflexive, symmetric and transitive (cf. the definitions of these properties given earlier in this section).

For any $a \in A$ the subset of A

$$[a]_R = \{b \mid a R b\}$$

is called an **equivalence class** of R in A. By $A/_R$ we denote the set of all equivalence classes of R in A. As is easy to see, if a R b, then $[a]_R = [b]_R$ and otherwise $[a]_R \cap [b]_R = \phi$. Equivalence classes constitute a so called **partition** of the set A, i.e. such a class of mutually disjoint nonempty subsets of A whose union equals A. Conversely every partition in A unambiguously defines an equivalence relation in A.

Let $f : A \times ... \times A \rightarrow A$ be a n-argument total function in A and let R be an equivalence relation in A. We say that R is a **congruence** wrt f in A if

$a_1 R b_1$ **and** ... **and** $a_n R b_n$
   implies
$f.\langle a_1,...,a_n \rangle R f.\langle b_1,...b_n \rangle$

In that case we can construct a function

$$f/_R : A/_R \times ... \times A/_R \rightarrow A/_R$$

defined by the following equation:

$$f/_R.[a]_R = [f.a]_R$$

Observe that this definition is unambiguous only because R is a congruence.

The simplest example of a congruence relation is, of course, an equality relation. A less trivial example is the equivalence of regular expressions (two regular expressions are equivalent if they denote the same language) with respect to the usual operations on these expressions.

FUNCTIONS

Functions play a central role in denotational semantics since in general the definition of a software system consists in its major part of several definitions of functions. After having defined the syntactic and the semantic domains we define operations on data, which are functions, the denotations of expressions, commands, etc., which are functions again, and finally a tuple of functions which describe the semantics of the system.

Functions in denotational semantics are most frequently defined in a constructive way, i.e. as combinations of some previously defined functions. In this and in the next section we discuss two different techniques which are used in such definitions. We start from an intuitive characterization of both of them.

In the first case functions are constructed on the ground of a calculus of functions derived from the calculus of relations (Sec.3). E.g. we define a function $f:A \to A$ as a sequential composition of $g:A \to A$ and $h:A \to A$

$$f = g \cdot h \qquad\qquad (4.1)$$

or as the least solution of an equation:

$$f = (id.B) \cdot h \cdot f \mid (id.(A-B)) \qquad\qquad (4.2)$$

where $B \subseteq A$. Within that technique a function is defined by an expression which gives that function as a resulting value, or by a fixed point equation where this function is the least solution or by a set of fixed point equations in a case of mutual recursion (cf. Sec.2).

In the other case functions are defined by equations of the form:

f.a = "an expression where "a" is an argument"

where the right—hand—side expression describes the way of calculating
the value of f for an arbitrary argument a. Definitions written in
that style are similar to functional—procedure declarations, where
the argument   a   plays   the   role of a formal parameter. Of course,
every definition written in the former style may be translated into
the latter style. For instance, the definitions (4.1) and (4.2)
become:

f.a = h.(g.a) $\qquad\qquad$ (4.3)

and respectively

$$f.a = a\epsilon B \rightarrow f.(h.a),$$
$$a\cancel{\epsilon}B \rightarrow a \qquad\qquad (4.4)$$

Definitions written in the calculus of   functions   are called
definitions with hidden arguments whereas the others are called
definitions with formal parameters. Definitions with   hidden
arguments are very transparent — if not too long — and are convenient
in the proofs of certain properties of functions such as e.g.
continuity or assertion—correctness.   The   other style is more
advisable when we define curried functions of complex types and is —
informally speaking — more "operationally oriented". That style is
closer to our intuition when we think of denotational definitions as
of programs written in a functional   programming   language and
representing the interpreters of defined systems.

Definitions with formal parameters constitute   essentially   a
modification of definitions written in a so called **calculus of
lambda—expressions.** In the latter the definitions of functions have
the following form:

f = (λa)("an expression where "a" is an argument").

For instance, (4.4) written in lambda—expression style is as follows:

$$f = (\lambda a) \ (a\epsilon B \rightarrow f.(h.a),$$
$$a\cancel{\epsilon}B \rightarrow a)$$

In this book we shall most frequently use formal-parameter notation rather than lambda-expression notation. The latter will be used only occasionally.

The formal-parameter style will be fully discussed in the next section. Here we shall concentrate on the calculus of functions which we derive from the previously defined calculus of relations. We start by recalling three major types of cpo's of functions which the reader already knows from Sec.2.

The cpo of partial functions. Given two arbitrary sets A and B the pair $\langle A\tilde{\to}B, \subseteq \rangle$ constitutes a cpo where $A\tilde{\to}B$ denotes the set of all partial functions from A into B and $\subseteq$ denotes the set-theoretic inclusion of functions. The ordering $\subseteq$ is called the **horizontal ordering** of partial functions.

The cpo of total functions. Given a set A and a cpo $\langle B, \sqsubseteq_B \rangle$ the pair $\langle A\to B, \sqsubseteq \rangle$ constitutes a cpo, where $A\to B$ denotes the set of all total functions from A into B and where $\sqsubseteq$ denotes an argumentwise ordering induced in $A\to B$ by $\sqsubseteq_B$ in the following way:

$$f \sqsubseteq g \quad \text{iff} \quad f.a \sqsubseteq_B g.a \quad \text{for all } a\varepsilon A.$$

The ordering $\sqsubseteq$ is called the **vertical ordering** of total functions.

The cpo of continuous functions. Given two cpo's $\langle A, \sqsubseteq_A \rangle$ and $\langle B, \sqsubseteq_B \rangle$ the pair $\langle A\underset{c}{\to}B, \sqsubseteq \rangle$ constitutes a cpo where $A\underset{c}{\to}B$ denotes the set of all continuous functions from $\langle A, \sqsubseteq_A \rangle$ into $\langle B, \sqsubseteq_B \rangle$ and where $\sqsubseteq$ denotes the vertical ordering between such functions.

For any two sets (respectively cpo's) A and B we obviously have the following inclusions between the corresponding sets of functions and relations:

$$A\underset{c}{\to}B \subseteq A\to B \subseteq A\tilde{\to}B \subseteq Rel.\langle A.B\rangle$$

This means that all operations on relations – in particular all operations which have been defined in Sec.3 – are applicable to functions. On the other hand, not all of them preserve the functionality, the totality or the continuity of their arguments. Below we define some most frequently used operations which preserve functionality. Later we shall discuss their applicability to total and continuous functions.

Sequential composition. For any $f:A \to B$ and $g:C \to D$, by $f \cdot g$ we denote the composition of f and g defined exactly as in Sec.3. Of course, $f \cdot g$ is a partial function from A into D, i.e. $f \cdot g:A \to D$.

Similarly as in the case of relations we usually write fg for $f \cdot g$. Also, since our operation is associative, we write fgh rather than $(fg)h$ or $f(gh)$. A composition of a function f and a set A is denoted by fA or Af respectively. $id.A$ denotes the identity function on A and ϕ denotes the empty function.

Notice that in fg we first "perform" f and then g, i.e. $(fg).a = g.(f.a)$. We have chosen this notation since it is compatible with the usual order of execution in programs and therefore leads to more natural semantic clauses. E.g. a clause which defines the composition of commands has the following form:

$$C[com_1;com_2] = C[com_1] \cdot C[com_2]$$

rather than $C[com_1;com_2] = C[com_2] \cdot C[com_1]$.

The other operations on relations defined in Sec.3, although formally applicable to functions do not always return functions as values. For instance, the union of two functions, or an iteration of a function need not to be a function. On the other hand these operation may still be used in the definitions of functions. For instance, if h is a function, then the least solution of the equation (4.2) which may be expressed by

$$f = [(id.B)h]^* id.(A-B)$$

is a function. Below we define a few further operations on functions.

Conditional union. For every $p:A \to B$ and $f,g:A \to C$ we define the following function in $A \to C$:

IF p **THEN** f **ELSE** g **FI** =
  (id.{a| p.a=tt})f | (id.{a| p.a=ff})g

In applications tt (true) and ff (false) usually belong to B but formally we do not require this in our definition. We also do not exclude the case where B contains elements different from tt or ff such as e.g. abstract errors. Of course, if tt,ff∉B, then **IF** p **THEN** f **ELSE** g **FI** = φ. If A = C and g = id.A, then we use an abbreviated notation: **IF** p **THEN** f **FI**.

The reader may have the impression that our definition of conditional union could have been written in the following more intuitive form:

  IF p **THEN** f **ELSE** g **FI**.a =
    p.a=tt → f.a,
    p.a=ff → g.a,
    TRUE   → ?

where "?" stands for "undefined". The reason why we do not want to write our definition in such a form is the following. First, this definition uses "?" as a value which is not acceptable in our formalism. Second, it refers to "→" which has been introduced, so far, only intuitively. The meaning of "→" will be formalized in the next section in the terms of conditional union. The latter must, therefore, be defined independently. In the present section we define the calculus of functions on the ground of the earlier defined calculus of relations which, in turn, was defined in set theory. We allow ourselves for the use of "→" in intuitive comments and in examples, but we refrain from using it in formal definitions until it is formally introduced in Sec.5.

Overwriting. For every f:A⇸B and g:C⇸D we define the following function in (A|C)⇸(B|D):

  f[g] = g | (id.(A−dom.g))f

The function f[g] behaves like g wherever g is defined and everywhere else behaves like f. In other words

  f[g].a = a ε dom.g → g.a,
           a ∉ dom.g → f.a

Observe that if dom.g n dom.f = φ, then f[g] = f|g. It is also easy to prove that overwriting is associative. We assume that overwriting binds stronger than the application of an argument to a function, i.e. that f.g[h] means f.(g[h]).

Restriction. For any f:A⇸B and C we define the following function in C⇸B:

$$f \setminus C = (id.C)f$$

For technical convenience we also introduce the following operation of removing an element from the domain of a function:

$$f[?/a] = f \setminus ((dom.f) - \{a\})$$

The reader may easily check that all operations defined in this section preserve the functionality of their arguments. They may be regarded, therefore, as operations defined in the cpo's of functions. Let us discuss their continuity property in each of the cpo's of functions which we have introduced earlier.

In the cpo's of partial functions with horizontal ordering the operations of composition, conditional union and restriction, the latter regarded as a one-argument function of f, are continuous in all arguments. The operation of overwriting is continuous only in f, since in g it is not monotone. Moreover, restriction is continuous in C whenever C ranges over a cpo of sets ordered by inclusion and with the least upper bounds equal to unions. The reader may wish to show that if C ranges over a cpo where lub's are different from unions, then f\C is not continuous in C.

In order to discuss the continuity of functional constructors in the cpo of total functions we first have to adjust their definitions in such a way that they always lead from total to total functions and that the bottom element plays the role of an "undefinedness". For f:A→B and g:B→C we set:

$$f \bullet g = \{\langle a, g.(f.a)\rangle \mid f.a \neq \bot_B\}$$
$$\mid \{\langle a, \bot_C\rangle \mid f.a = \bot_B\}$$

For technical simplicity we have assumed here that the codomain of f coincides with the domain of g. We shall assume similar simplifications for the remaining constructors. For p:A→B and f,g:A→C we set:

IF p **THEN** f **ELSE** g **FI** = {⟨a,f.a⟩ | p.a = tt}
  | {⟨a,g.a⟩ | p.a = ff}
  | {⟨a,⊥_C⟩ | p.a ∉ {tt,ff}}

For f:A→B, g:A→B and C ⊆ A we set:

f[g] = {⟨a,g.a⟩ | g.a ≠ ⊥_B}
  | {⟨a,f.a⟩ | g.a = ⊥_B}

f\C = {⟨a,f.a⟩ | a ε C}
  | {⟨a,⊥_B⟩ | a ∉ C}

The continuity properties of our constructors are now the following:

1. Composition is continuous in g but not continuous in f. The proof of the first fact is routine. To prove the second take a fixed nonmonotone g (notice that B and C are both cpo's) and observe that in this case f•g is nonmonotone in f and therefore cannot be continuous.

2. Conditional union is always continuous in f and g, and if the ordering in B is flat, then it is also continuous in p,. Proofs are routine. The reader may wish to check that the flatness of B is only a sufficient condition (but not necessary) for the continuity of our operator in p.

3. Overwriting is continuous in f but noncontinuous, since nonmonotone, in g.

4. Restriction is continuous in f and its continuity in C depends on the same condition as in the case of partial functions.

In the cpo of continuous functions we may only use composition and conditional union, and the latter only when B is flat (cf. Theorem 1.1.4.3), since in the other cases our constructors may lead from continuous to noncontinuous functions. Both, the composition and the conditional union are continuous in that cpo.

As a special case of partial functions we frequently use so called **mappings** i.e. functions with finite domains. By

$$A \xrightarrow[m]{} B$$

we denote the set of all mappings from A to B. Of course, A need not be finite, but for any $f:A\xrightarrow[m]{}B$, dom.f is finite. Mappings are partially ordered by inclusion, but that ordering is not complete. Since, however, mappings are finite objects, we never define mappings by fixed-point equations, and therefore the fact that $A\xrightarrow[m]{}B$ is not a cpo does not really matter.

Mappings are most frequently defined by an explicit enumeration. For any string $\langle b_1,\ldots,b_n\rangle$ and any repetition-free string $\langle a_1,\ldots,a_n\rangle$ by

$$[b_1/a_1,\ldots,b_n/a_n]$$

we denote a mapping such that

$$\text{dom.}[b_1/a_1,\ldots,b_n/a_n] = \{a_1,\ldots,a_n\} \quad \text{and}$$

$$[b_1/a_1,\ldots,b_n/a_n].a_i = b_i \quad \text{for} \quad i=1,\ldots,n$$

By [] we denote the **empty mapping**. If we overwrite a function by a mapping we use only one set of square brackets, e.g. we write f[b/a] rather than f[[b/a]].

A similar notation to that for mappings is used for **constant functions**. Of course the latter do not need to be finite. For any set A and any element b by

$$[b/a \mid a\varepsilon A]$$

we denote a total constant function in A with the value b.

THE DEFINITIONS OF FUNCTIONS WITH FORMAL PARAMETERS

The definitions of functions with formal parameters are similar to the declarations of functional procedures in programming languages. In the simplest case they are of the form

$$f.a = exp$$

where exp is an expression which describes the value of f in a. E.g. $f.a = 2a+3$. The argument a is then referred to as a **formal parameter** of the definition. In a more complex case, f may be a so called **curried function**, i.e.

$$f : A_1 \to (A_2 \to \ldots \to (A_{n-1} \to A_n) \ldots)$$

in which case the definition is of the form

$$f.a_1.a_2. \ldots .a_{n-1} = exp$$

This scheme may be further enriched by allowing that some formal parameters are given as so called **templates**, i.e. structure-reflexing expressions. E.g. in the definition of a concatenation of tuples

$$conc : Tuple \times Tuple \to Tuple$$

we may write

$$conc.\langle\langle a_1,\ldots,a_n\rangle,\langle b_1,\ldots,b_m\rangle\rangle =$$
$$\langle a_1,\ldots,a_n,b_1,\ldots,b_m\rangle$$

In this section we describe a notation used in the definitions of functions with formal parameters along with some principles of the construction of such definitions.

Function types. Every definition of a function — whether with hidden arguments or with formal parameters — should be preceded by a declaration, of the type of that function. E.g. if f is a total function from A to B, then the declaration of its type is of the form f:A→B, where

   dom.f = A and rng.f ⊆ B.

If f is a continuous function from a cpo A into a cpo B, then we write f:A⊆ₒB with the same requirements for dom.f and rng.f. If our function is partial, then we write f:A⇾B and require that dom.f ⊆ A and rng.f ⊆ B. We require the same for mappings in which case we write f:A⇾ₘB.

As we see, the type of a function is an attribute quite arbitrarily assigned by a declaration, rather than unambiguously defined by the function. Type declarations make the definitions of functions easier to read and may help in the identification of errors. In a formalized metalanguage they may be used by a static mechanism of error detection.

The sets A and B may be represented in a declaration either by simple names of domains, such as Real, Identifier, State, etc., or as so called **domain expressions** e.g of the form. RealxReal or State⇾State. Examples of the declarations of function types may be following:

       add : (Real x Real) → Real|{OVERFLOW}
    select : Array → Index → Element|{ERROR}
        C : Command → (State ⇾ State)

Curried functions. With every function of the type

   f : (A x B) ⇾ C

we may unambiguously associate a function

   F : A → (B ⇾ C)

which is called the **curried version** of f (after H.B.Curry, a British logician, cf. [Curry,Feys 58]) and which is defined in the following way:

$$(F.a).b = f.\langle a,b \rangle$$

In other words, for every $a \varepsilon A$, F.a is a partial function from B to C whose value for any $b \varepsilon B$ is $f.\langle a,b \rangle$. Of course, if $f.\langle a,b \rangle$ is undefined, then F.a is undefined in b. Note, however, that although f is partial, F is always a total function in A.

The operation of function curryfication may be generalized to functions of more than two-arguments. For every

$$f : A_1 \times \ldots \times A_n \mathrel{\ooalign{\raise0.3ex\hbox{$\not$}\cr$\to$}} C$$

we define

$$F : A_1 \to (A_2 \to \ldots \to (A_n \mathrel{\ooalign{\raise0.3ex\hbox{$\not$}\cr$\to$}} C)\ldots) \tag{5.1}$$

in an analogous way. Observe that in this case all the arrows but the last are total-function arrows "$\to$". The type of the last arrow is here the same as the type of the arrow in the declaration of f.

For simplicity of notation we omit parentheses in type-declarations of curried functions assuming that arrows associate to the right. Instead of (5.1) we write therefore

$$F : A_1 \to A_2 \to \ldots \to A_n \mathrel{\ooalign{\raise0.3ex\hbox{$\not$}\cr$\to$}} C$$

Sometimes we also deal with functions whose types are derived from curried types in replacing $\to$ by $\mathrel{\ooalign{\raise0.3ex\hbox{$\not$}\cr$\to$}}$, $\underset{c}{\to}$ or $\underset{m}{\to}$. E.g. we may define a function of the type:

$$g : A \mathrel{\ooalign{\raise0.3ex\hbox{$\not$}\cr$\to$}} B \underset{m}{\to} C$$

As we already assumed in Sec.2 we write f.a for f(a) and f.a.b.c for ((f.a).b).c. We use parentheses only in order to indicate some special arrangement of arguments. E.g. if we declare two functions

$$f : A \to B \to C \mathrel{\ooalign{\raise0.3ex\hbox{$\not$}\cr$\to$}} D \quad \text{and}$$
$$g : E \to B$$

then we may write f.a.(g.e).c.

As we shall see in the sequel, curried functions appear routinely in
denotational definitions. Typical examples are the functions of
semantics :

    E : Expression → State → Value|{ERROR}
    C : Command   → State ⇸ State
    P : Procedure → Parameter → State ⇸ State

In that case we make an exception in our notation. The first, i.e.
the "syntactic", argument of a function of semantics is always closed
in square brackets. E.g. we write E.[ide].sta or C.[ide:=exp].sta,
etc. This makes semantic clauses more readable and also coincides
with the traditional notation in denotational semantics.

Lambda expressions. In the definition of the form

    f.a = exp

exp is an expression which contains a free variable a and defines
the value of f in a. The same definition may be alternatively
written in the form

    f = (λx)exp

where (λx)exp is called a lambda expression. Since lambda
expressions denote functions we may write, e.g.:

    (λx)(2x+1) : Real → Real   or
    (λx)(2x+1).3 = 7

Lambda expressions may also be used to denote many—argument functions
or curried functions. E.g.

    ((λ⟨x,y⟩)(x+y) : Real × Real → Real   or
    (λx)((λy)(x+y)) : Real → Real → Real

Observe that in the second formula the expression which follows
(λx) is a lambda expression itself.

Lambda expressions have been formalized on the ground of a so called
lambda calculus (see e.g. [Stoy 1977] or [Barendregt 1984]). In
this book, however, we use lambda expressions only occasionally and
therefore we shall not explain the details of that formalism.

Conditional expressions. Expressions which stand on the right-hand
sides of the definitions of functions with formal parameters are most
frequently of the form:

$$p.a \to f.a, \ g.a \qquad\qquad (5.2)$$

where $p:A \to B$, $f,g:A \to C$ and where B is a set which contains the
truth values tt and ff plus possibly some other values such as
e.g. error messages. Formally (5.2) is understood as an alternative
notation for **IF** p **THEN** f **ELSE** g **FI**.a i.e.:

$$p.a \to f.a, \ g.a = IF \ p \ THEN \ f \ ELSE \ g \ FI.a$$

In every conditional expression both f.a and g.a may be replaced
either by constants or by other conditional expression. In the latter
case we most frequently use nested conditional expressions of the
form

$$p_1.a \to f_1.a, \ (\ldots,(p_n.a \to f_n.a, \ g.a)\ldots) \qquad\qquad (5.3)$$

which we write as a column of so called **conditional clauses**:

$$p_1.a \to f_1.a,$$
$$\cdot \ \cdot \ \cdot$$
$$p_n.a \to f_n.a,$$
$$TRUE \to g.a \qquad\qquad (5.4)$$

Sometimes instead of TRUE we write a formula which is logically
equivalent to $not(p_1.a \ or \ \ldots \ or \ p_n.a)$. E.g.

$$sgn.x = x>0 \to 1,$$
$$x=0 \to 0,$$
$$x<0 \to -1$$

In each conditional clause $p_i.a$ is called the **guard** and
$f_i.a$ is called the **guarded expression**. As follows from the

semantics of (5.3), the order in which we write its conditional clauses is relevant to its meaning. See the following example. Let

$$Real = \{a \mid m \leqslant abs.a \leqslant M\} \mid \{0\}$$

be the set of machine-representable reals, and let us define a function "the square of an inverse"

$$sqin : Real \rightarrow Real \mid \{OVERFLOW\}$$

$$sqin.r =$$
$$\quad r=0 \qquad\qquad \rightarrow OVERFLOW,$$
$$\quad m \leq (1/r)^2 \leq M \rightarrow (1/r)^2,$$
$$\quad TRUE \qquad\qquad \rightarrow OVERFLOW$$

The defined function is, of course, total in Real. Now observe that if we permute the first clause with the second, i.e. if we set

$$sqin.r =$$
$$\quad m \leq (1/r)^2 \leq M \rightarrow (1/r)^2,$$
$$\quad r=0 \qquad\qquad \rightarrow OVERFLOW,$$
$$\quad TRUE \qquad\qquad \rightarrow OVERFLOW$$

then the new function is undefined for r=0 since the first guard is undefined in that case.

Let clauses. The readability of complex definitions may be frequently improved by introducing a local variable to denote a value which is used more than once and/or which is defined by a long expression. For that sake we use the notation of the form

$$\textbf{let } x=exp_1 \textbf{ in } exp_2$$

where exp_1 and exp_2 may be arbitrary expressions. In evaluating **let** $x=exp_1$ **in** exp_2 we first evaluate exp_1 and if that value is defined, then we substitute it for x in the evaluation of exp_2. In the terms of λ-calculus we may say that we evaluate

$$((\lambda x)exp_2).exp_1$$

If x appears in exp_1 and we wish to indicate that x is being defined as the least solution of

$$x = exp_1$$

where the corresponding cpo must be clear from the type of exp_1, then we write:

letrec $x=exp_1$ **in** exp_2

If we wish to define two or more local objects by a mutual fixed—point recursion, then we put the entire corresponding set of fixed—point equations (separated by commas) into one **letrec**-clause. This construction is also legal if x_i's do not appear in the exp_i's. In that case we have a trivial recursion, but the corresponding least fixed point is calculated anyway, i.e. all corresponding assignments are performed "in parallel" rather than one after another. In a multiple **letrec**-clause we do not need, of course, to care about the order of clauses.

We also allow non—recursive compound **let**-clauses. In that case, however, whether we put several equations into one clause or into separate clauses makes no difference for the meaning. And, of course, now the order of clauses matters again.

Expressions with let—clauses are allowed as subexpressions of other expressions. In particular, both exp_1 and exp_2 may contain their own local **let**-clauses.

If a let—clause defines a local function, then it may be of the form $f.x = exp_1$ or, in general, of any form which is allowed for function definitions with parameters. Recursion is allowed in that case as well. The following is a simple example of a definition with let—clauses:

$$E.[(exp_1 \ \underline{plus} \ exp_2)].sta =$$
    let $val_1 = E[exp_1].sta$ **in**
    $val_1\varepsilon Error \rightarrow val_1,$
    let $val_2 = E[exp_2].sta$ **in**
    $val_2\varepsilon Error \rightarrow val_2,$
    TRUE $\rightarrow plus.\langle val_1, val_2\rangle$ (5.5)

Templates. In dealing with functions whose arguments are tuples or mappings it is convenient to express in the notation the structure of such arguments. E.g. we may wish to define a function of the type

$$f : (A \times B) \times C \to A \times B \times C$$

such that:

$$f.\langle\langle a,b\rangle,c\rangle = \langle a,b,c\rangle$$

or to define a function g on mappings such that:

$$f.[a/x,b/y,c/z] = [b/x,a/y,c/z]$$

Formulas which represent structured arguments are called **templates**. Beside tuple- or mapping-templates we also frequently use templates which represent elements of some syntactic domains. This is typically the case in the definitions of the functions of semantics. E.g. in (5.5) $(exp_1 \text{ plus } exp_2)$ is such a template.

Templates may also be used at the left-hand sides of let-clauses. E.g. we may write

$$\textbf{let } \langle\langle a,b\rangle,c\rangle = tuple \textbf{ in } exp \tag{5.6}$$

by which we mean that exp is evaluated in an environment where the variables a, b and c were given the values of the corresponding components of the value of the expression "tuple". If the value of that expression does not match the structure of the template, then the value of the whole expression (5.6) is undefined.

Special cases are templates which represent a scheme of a structure. For instance, if the value of the expression "tuple" may be of a varying length, then we may write

$$\textbf{let } \langle a_1,\ldots,a_n\rangle = tuple \textbf{ in } exp$$

In that case we assume that the "elaboration" of the let-clause results in the association of the corresponding tuple to the variable a and of the length of that tuple to the variable n. Later in the evaluation of exp each a_i with $1 \leq i \leq n$ denotes the i-th element of a.

We do not allow clauses of the form

    let $\{a_1,...,a_n\}$ = set **in** exp

since at the level of our meta-semantics this would lead to the necessity of choosing an a priori order in a given set.

Most frequently templates correspond to tuples, mappings and their combinations. We shall not try to formalize here what may and what may not be a template. As long as we only introduce a notation, rather than a formalized metalanguage, we allow here any mathematical expression which makes sense. We should only stress in this place that the use of templates with "...", or in general the use of "..." in any other context must be rigidly formalized before denotational definitions may be "semantically processed" by a computer.

Split definitions. The number of conditional clauses in certain definitions of functions may be very large. For instance, in the definitions of a functions of semantics that number equals to the number of possible templates which the corresponding syntactic argument may match. This usually leads to a few tens of cases. In order to make such definitions readable we usually describe each of its cases by a separate equation. For instance, we may have the following equations in a definition of a function of semantics of expressions:

    E[ide].sta = ...
    E[<u>not</u> exp].sta = ...
    E[(exp_1 <u>less</u> exp_2)].sta = ...
    E[(exp_1 <u>plus</u> exp_2)].sta = ...

TUPLES, STRINGS AND CARTESIAN OPERATIONS

By a **tuple** we mean a mapping from a set of the form $\{1,\ldots,n\}$ into another set. To denote a tuple we use angle-parenthesis:

$$\langle a_1,\ldots,a_n \rangle = [a_1/1,\ldots,a_n/n]$$

Empty tuple is, of course, just the empty mapping and is denoted by:

$$\langle\rangle = [\,]$$

The **Cartesian product** of sets $A_1,\ldots,A_n$ with $n \geq 2$ is understood as a set of tuples:

$$A_1 \times \ldots \times A_n = \{\langle a_1,\ldots,a_n \rangle \mid a_i \varepsilon A_i \quad \text{for} \quad i \leq n\}$$

It should be emphasized that for any $n \geq 2$ we define here a separate operation of a Cartesian product of n sets. This is due to the fact, that the Cartesian product of two sets is not associative, i.e.

$$(A \times B) \times C \neq A \times (B \times C)$$

and therefore

$$A_1 \times \ldots \times A_n \neq A_1 \times (A_2 \times \ldots \times A_n)$$

for $n \geq 3$.

Of course, in many mathematical textbooks Cartesian product is "assumed to be associative". This assumption means that one agrees to identify the tuples $\langle\langle a,b \rangle,c \rangle$, $\langle a,\langle b,c \rangle\rangle$ and $\langle a,b,c \rangle$. It is rather clear that in our applications we do not want to identify such tuples.

For any set A   we define a **Cartesian power** and two **Cartesian iterations** of   A:

$$A^{c0} = \{<>\} \qquad\qquad\qquad \text{null Cartesian power}$$
$$A^{cn} = \{<a_1,\ldots,a_n> \mid a_i \varepsilon A\} \quad \text{n-th Cartesian power for } n\geq 1$$
$$A^{c+} = U_{n=1}^{\infty} A^{cn} \qquad\qquad \text{Cartesian-plus iteration}$$
$$A^{c\star} = U_{n=0}^{\infty} A^{cn} \qquad\qquad \text{Cartesian-star iteration}$$

The operations of Cartesian powers and iterations must not be confused with the analogous operations on formal languages (cf. Sec.7). In particular, several equalities commonly known from the theory of formal languages do not hold here, e.g.:

$$A^{c1} \neq A$$
$$A^{c0} \times A \neq A \neq A \times A^{c0}$$
$$A^{cn} \times A \neq A^{c(n+1)} \neq A \times A^{cn}$$
$$A^{c\star} \times A \neq A^{c+} \neq A \times A^{c\star}$$

In every set of tuples $A^{c\star}$ we define the following operations:

Selection. This is an operation which given a tuple of length $n\geq 1$ and an integer (index) $1\leq i\leq n$ returns the i-th element of that tuple. Since tuples are functions (mappings)   on indices, the selection operation is nothing else but the application of a tuple to an index:

$$<a_1,\ldots,a_n>.i = a_i \qquad \text{for} \qquad 1\leq i\leq n \tag{6.1}$$

First, tail, last, cotail. For every nonempty tuple $<a_1,..,a_n>$ we define

$$\text{first.}<a_1,\ldots,a_n> = a_1$$
$$\text{tail.}<a_1,\ldots,a_n> = <a_2,\ldots,a_n>$$
$$\text{last.}<a_1,\ldots,a_n> = a_n$$
$$\text{cotail.}<a_1,\ldots,a_n> = <a_1,\ldots,a_{n-1}>$$

It is understood that for n=1, $<a_2,\ldots,a_n>=<>=<a_1,\ldots,a_{n-1}>$. We also assume that for an empty argument all these funtions are undefined.

Here one side remark is in order. The definition (6.1) should not be

misunderstood by assuming that the subscripts of literals which
denote the elements of a tuple must coincide with the indices of
these elements. In fact, indices always define the position of an
element in a tuple and subscripts do not need to correspond to them.
For instance:

$$\langle a_2,\ldots,a_n\rangle.1 = a_2$$
$$\langle a_2,\ldots,a_n\rangle.2 = a_3$$
$$\langle a_9,a_7,b,c\rangle.1 = a_9 \qquad \text{etc.}$$

Concatenation. This is an operation which "glues" any two tuples
together:

1) $\langle\rangle^\wedge\langle\rangle = \langle\rangle$
2) $\langle\rangle^\wedge\langle b_1,\ldots,b_n\rangle = \langle b_1,\ldots,b_n\rangle^\wedge\langle\rangle = \langle b_1,\ldots,b_n\rangle$
3) $\langle a_1,\ldots,a_n\rangle^\wedge\langle b_1,\ldots,b_m\rangle =$
   $\langle a_1,\ldots,a_n,b_1,\ldots,b_m\rangle$

The concatenation of tuples is, of course, associative and the empty
tuple $\langle\rangle$ is the unit of that operation.

Repetition-free. This is a predicate defined as follows:

$$\text{repetition-free} : A^{C^*} \rightarrow \{tt,ff\}$$

$$\text{repetition-free}.\langle a_1,\ldots,a_n\rangle =$$
$$(\exists j,k\leq n)(j\neq k \text{ and } a_j=a_k) \rightarrow ff, tt$$

Tuples are otherwise called **finite strings**. Beside finite strings
we also introduce **infinite strings** for which we use the notation:

$$\langle a_1,a_2,\ldots\rangle$$

and which we define as total functions from the set of positive
integers $Pint=\{1,2,\ldots\}$ into another set. For any set A we
define:

$$A^{C^\infty} = Pint \rightarrow A$$
$$A^{C\omega} = A^{C+} \mid A^{C^\infty}$$

The operations "first", "tail" and "repetition-free" are now generalized to $A^{c\omega}$ in an obvious way. The operation of concatenation is generalized as follows:

4) $\langle\rangle^\wedge\langle b_1,b_2,\ldots\rangle = \langle b_1,b_2,\ldots\rangle$

5) $\langle a_1,\ldots,a_n\rangle^\wedge\langle b_1,b_2,\ldots\rangle =$
   $\langle a_1,\ldots,a_n,b_1,b_2,\ldots\rangle$

6) $\langle b_1,b_2,\ldots\rangle^\wedge s = \langle b_1,b_2,\ldots\rangle$ for any $s\varepsilon A^{c\omega}|\{\langle\rangle\}$

FORMAL LANGUAGES

The theory of formal languages provides mathematical techniques used
in the definitions of the syntax of programming languages. In this
section we do not intend to describe these techniques neither to
summarize the theory. A familiarity with formal languages is one of
the prerequisites for this book. We restrict ourselves to the
introduction of a notation and we add some comments about the
fixed-point definitions of context-free languages. We also briefly
discuss languages with infinite words.

By an **alphabet** we mean a nonempty, usually finite, set. By a
formal language or simply a **language** over an alphabet   A   we mean
any subset of A^{c^*}. By

$$Lan.A = \{L \mid L \subseteq A^{c^*}\}$$

we denote the set of all languages over A. The **concatenation of
languages** is defined in the usual way:

$$L_1 {}^{\char94} L_2 = \{t_1 {}^{\char94} t_2 \mid t_1 \varepsilon L_1 \text{ **and** } t_2 \varepsilon L_2\}$$

If this leads to no confusion, then we omit the sign "^" and write
simply $L_1 L_2$. In   Lan.A we define the operation of **concatenation
power** and two operations of **concatenation iteration**. Let $L \varepsilon Lan.A$:

$$L^0 = \{<>\} \qquad \text{null concatenation power}$$
$$L^n = LL^{n-1} \quad \text{for} \quad n \geq 1 \quad \text{n-th concatenation power}$$
$$L^+ = \textstyle\bigcup_{n=1}^{\infty} L^n \qquad \text{concatenation-plus iteration}$$
$$L^* = \textstyle\bigcup_{n=0}^{\infty} L^n \qquad \text{concatenation-star iteration}$$

Notice the difference between concatenation operation and the
corresponding Cartesian operations defined in Sec.6:

1) Cartesian operations are applicable to any sets whereas

concatenation operations are applicable only to languages.

2) Concatenation is associative whereas Cartesian product is not.

3) For any $L \in Lan.A$, L^* is a set of tuples whose elements belong to A whereas L^{c*} is a set of tuples whose elements belong to L.

Now let us show a typical example of the application of "c*" and explain why "*" cannot be used in its place. Assume that we are designing a word processor, where we define four following domains:

```
Character       = {a,b,...}
Document        = Character^{c*}
Document-stack  = Document^{c*}
Memory          = Identifier →_m Document-stack
```

Since on the ground of our approach we wish to distinguish between an element a and a one-element tuple <a> the set Character cannot be regarded as a set of tuples and therefore the operation "*" does not apply to it. In order to define the set Document we have to use "c*". Now we define Document-stack. Although Document is a set of tuples and therefore "*" applies to it, we cannot use this operation in our definition since $Document^* = Document$. What we want to define is a set of tuples of documents. Each such a tuple represents a sequence of successive editions of a document and is assigned to the name (identifier) of that document in the memory. In order to define Document-stack we have to use "c*" again.

For every alphabet A the pair $(Lan.A, \subseteq)$ constitutes a set-theoretic cpo. All our operations on languages, plus the operation of union, are continuous in that cpo. Using these operations and fixed-point techniques one can define any context-free language (cf.[Blikle 72a]).

Besides classical formal languages we also use so called **generalized formal languages** with possibly infinite words. They are most frequently applied in a so called **trace semantics** in describing the effect of nonterminating computations. By

$$Genlan.A = \{L \mid L \subseteq A^{c\omega}\} \mid \{<>\}$$

we denote the set of all generalized languages over A. In a way analogous as before we define in that set the operations of concatenation, power and both iterations. As is easy to check, all these operations are continuous in the cpo $\langle \text{Genlan.A}, \subseteq \rangle$. For any generalized language L we define two infinitary iterations of that language:

$$L^{\infty}$$

to be the greatest solution of the equation $X = LX$, and

$$L^{\omega}$$

to be the greatest solution of the equation $X = L \mid LX$. As is easy to show

$$L^{\omega} = L^{+} \mid L^{\infty}$$

None of these infinitary operations is continuous in the cpo of generalized languages.

DOMAINS

Sets which appear in the denotational definitions of software systems are traditionally called **domains**. This term has been introduced to denotational semantics by Dana Scott who has used it to name special cpo's (see [Scott 1976]). In this book we shall use the word "domain" as a synonym of "set".

Domains in denotational semantics may be split into basically two groups. The first group contains formal languages which are otherwise called **syntactic domains** or **concrete syntactic domains**. As is well known, syntactic domains are constructed on the ground of a cpo of formal languages $\langle \text{Lan.A}, \subseteq \rangle$, where A is an appropriate alphabet.

Domains which belong to the other group are sometimes called **semantic domains**, although this term also covers abstract-syntactic domains and generalized languages. Typical semantic domains are the domains of data such as e.g.

```
Boolean   = {tt,ff}
Integer   = {i | m≤i≤M}
Character = {a,b,c,...,A,B,C,...}
Value     = Boolean | Integer | Character | Record
Record    = Identifier →ₘ Value
```

domains used to model machine states such as e.g.

```
Environment = Identifier →ₘ Location
Store       = Location →ₘ Value
State       = Environment × Store
```

the domains of denotations such as e.g.

```
Expression-denotation = State → Value|{ERROR}
Command-denotation    = State|{ERROR} →̃ State{ERROR}
```

$$\text{Declaration-denotation} = \text{State}|\{\text{ERROR}\} \rightarrow \text{State}|\{\text{ERROR}\}$$

and finally different auxiliary domains which we construct in order to simplify the definitions of the "main" domains.

In every denotational model of a software system semantic domains are constructed from some primitive domains such as e.g. Boolean, Integer or Character by using domain constructors such as $|$, $\times$, $\overset{*}{}$, $\rightarrow$, $\vec{m}$, etc. and possibly fixed-point techniques. For instance, in our example the defining equations of Value and Record involve fixed-point recursion.

If we are going to define domains by fixed-point equations we have to establish a cpo of domains and to check which of our domain constructors are continuous. A construction which we carry out in that case is analogous to the construction of a cpo of formal languages.

We start from establishing a family **B** of **basic domains**. This family plays an analogous role to that of an alphabet A in $\langle \text{Lan.A}, \subseteq \rangle$. Similarly to A, which we normally choose having a particular language in mind, the choice of **B** depends on the denotational model which we are going to construct. Typically **B** will contain such primitive domains as Boolean, Integer, Real, Identifier, Location, etc.

Given a family **B** we construct a set Dom.**B** of domains over **B**. This is a so called **universal set** in the sense of [Cohn 1981]. It contains the empty domain ϕ, all the domains of **B** and is closed under all typical domain operations and under the unions of enumerable subfamilies of **B**. It does not need however, to be closed under the unions of its arbitrary subfamilies. Since the construction of Dom.**B** is mathematically rather subtle we shall not explain it here. It is only important for us that the elements of Dom.**B** are ordinary sets (rather than cpo's, complete lattices or retracts (cf. [Scott 1976]) and that the equality between the elements of Dom.**B** is an ordinary equality of sets, rather than an isomorphism of lattices as in the approach of D.Scott. Details may be found in [Blikle,Tarlecki 1983].

Since Dom.**B** contains the empty set and is closed under the unions of enumerable families of sets it constitutes a set-theoretic cpo

(Dom.**B**,).   Below   we   list   most   frequently   used   operations   on domains and we discuss their continuity properties:

1)	A|B	the union of A and B
2)	AnB	the intersection of A and B
3)	$A_1 \times \ldots \times A_n$	the Cartesian product of $A_1, \ldots, A_n$
4)	A^{c0}	the null Cartesian power of A
5)	A^{cn}	the n-th Cartesian power of A
6)	A^{c+}	the Cartesian plus iteration of A
7)	A^{c*}	the Cartesian star iteration of A
8)	A-**finset**	the set of all finite subsets of A
9)	$A \xrightarrow{m} B$	the set of all mappings from A to B
10)	A-B	the difference of A and B
11)	A-**set**	the set of all subsets of A
12)	$A^{c\infty}$	the set of all infinite strings over A
13)	$A^{c\omega}$	the set of all finite and infinite strings over A
14)	$A \rightsquigarrow B$	the set of all partial functions from A to B
15)	A→B	the set of all total functions from A to B
16)	Rel.<A,B>	the set of all relations from A to B

As is easy to show (proofs are left to the reader) operations 1)–9) are continuous, the operation 10) is continuous only in A and the operations 11)–16) are non-continuous in all arguments. Consequently 1)–9) can be freely used in fixed-point domain equations, 10) may only be used if B represents a constant and 11)–16) may be used only in non-recursive equations.

Consider   as   an   example   the   following   set   of   recursive   domain equations:

```
Data    = Boolean | Integer
Value   = Data | Record | File
File    = Value^c*
Record  = Identifier →m Value
```

This set has a solution since all operations involved in the recursion between Value, File and Record are continuous. Now consider the set:

```
State                  = Identifier →m Value
Value                  = Integer | Record
Record                 = State
Expression-denotation  = State → (Value | {ERROR})
Command-denotation     = State ↝ State
```

This set also has a solution - although → and ↝ are not continuous - since the loop of recursive references (State→Value→Record→State) does not contain these domain names who's definitions involve noncontinuous functions. An example of a set which has no solution may be the following:

```
Value     = Boolean | Integer | Procedure
Procedure = State ↝ State
State     = Identifier →m Value
```

Here we have a mutual recursion with a non-continuous operation "↝". Of course, the fact that the described attempt to define procedures is a failure does not mean that storable procedures cannot be defined in our framework (see [Blikle,Tarlecki 83]). We should add in this palce that for any set of domain equations one can effectively construct all its loops of recursive references and therefore one can effectively check if they involve only continuous operations. This is a sufficient condition for the existence of solutions.

All operations 1)-16) are total functions in Dom.**B**. In other words, they are all applicable to all domains. Beside total operations we also use partial operations on domains. Typical examples are all operations on languages and generalized languages. If an alphabet A is an element of **B**, then Genlan.A ⊆ Dom.**B** and therefore every operation in Lan.A may be regarded as a partial operation in Dom.**B**.

Another example of a partial operation on domains is "→c". As we remember from Sec.4 if A and B are cpo's, then

$$A \underset{c}{\to} B \tag{8.1}$$

denotes the set of all continuous functions from A to B. Formally "→c" should be regarded as a partial four-argument operation in Dom.B, where instead of (8.1) we write

$$(A,P) \underset{C}{\rightarrow} (B,R) \qquad\qquad\qquad (8.2)$$

and require that for this domain to be defined the following conditions must be satisfied:

1) $P \subseteq A \times A$ and $R \subseteq B \times B$,
2) (A,P) and (B,R) are cpo's.

The last partial operation on domains which we include in our repertoire of domain constructors is defined via the operation of overwriting (Sec.4). Given two domains of partial functions $Fun_1 \subseteq A \stackrel{*}{\rightarrow} B$ and $Fun_2 \subseteq C \stackrel{*}{\rightarrow} D$ we define:

$$Fun_1 ! Fun_2 = \{f_1[f_2] \mid f_i \varepsilon Fun_i \quad for \quad i=1,2\}$$

Similarly to overwriting also "!" is associative. Observe also that if A is disjoint with C, then "!" is commutative since in that case $f_1[f_2] = f_1 | f_2$. Given an arbitrary family of functional domains $\{Fun_i \mid i \varepsilon I\}$ where $Fun_i \subseteq A_i \stackrel{*}{\rightarrow} B_i$ and A_i's are mutually disjoint we define:

$$!\{Fun_i \mid i \varepsilon I\} = \{Uf_i \mid f_i \varepsilon Fun_i \quad for \quad i \varepsilon I\}$$

Since for partial functions the property of continuity is meaningless we do not discuss that issue for our partial domain constructors.

We shall complete this section with the description of a few notational conventions for domains. The first of them concerns the priorities of domain constructors. We shall assume that all functional–domain constructors, i.e. $\rightarrow$, $\stackrel{*}{\rightarrow}$ and $\stackrel{\cdot}{\underset{m}{\rightarrow}}$ have lower priorities (are binding weaker) then all other constructors. We also assume that "|" is weaker then "x" and all iterations. No other priorities are assumed.

In defining a domain it is frequently convenient to simultaneously introduce a variable which ranges over the elements of that domain. Here we adopt a convention introduced in [Tennent 1976] where a domain equation may be preceded by a prefix which declares such a variable. For instance we write:

```
    ide : Identifier  = ...
    int : Integer     = ...
  s-env : Static-env  = ...
```

to indicate that an identifier, an integer or a static environment
will be denoted respectively by ide, int and s-env possibly with
indices. The names of domains always start with capital letters
whereas the names of their elements start with lower-case letters and
mimic the corresponding names of domains.

In some applications we use domains with elements labeled by the
names of these domains. For instance, if we define

```
  Bool = {0,1}
  Num  = {0,1,2,...}
```

and if then we want to define a domain of **values** which are either
boolean elements or numerals, we must "make these two former domains
disjoint". A standard way of doing that is to label each element of
each domain with the name of that domain. This labeling is made
implicit in the following notation for domain equations, where f
denotes a function on domains:

$$D :: f.\langle D_1,\dots,D_n \rangle$$

by which we mean that all elements of D are of the form
mk-"D-label".d, where $d \varepsilon f.\langle D_1,\dots,D_n \rangle$, and where D-label denotes
the name of D starting from a lower case letter. For instance, if we
define:

```
  Bool  :: {0,1}
  Num   :: {0,1,2,...}
  Value =  Bool | Num
```

then the elements of Bool are mk-bool.0 and mk-bool.1, and the
elements of Num are mk-num.0, mk-num.1, mk-num.3, etc. In the domain
Value we now may distinguish between the citizens of a boolean and of
a numeric origin. Of course, if we want to use a boolean-origin value
in the place where a boolean value is expected, e.g. as an argument
of the logical operator **not**, then we must remove the label. This
concerns any elements of labeled domains.

THREE—VALUED PREDICATES

> "... *everywhere in mathematics, the*
> *explicit formulation marks only the*
> *end of a sometimes long period of*
> *non-formulated operativeness, and in*
> *such a period the student must read in*
> *the teachers' face what his mind knows*
> *only semiconsciously."*
>
> [Freudental 73]

Predicates, i.e. functions which assume boolean values tt and ff, play a significant role in programming and in the formal definitions of software systems. They appear as the guards of conditional clauses (Sec.5), they are used to impose constraints on domains (such as e.g. the well—formedness of states), they serve to express the properties of software and last but not least they are used in axiomatic specifications.

On the ground of classical logic predicates are always regarded as total functions with only two possible values: "true" and "false". This is frequently expressed in colloquial terms by saying that every indicative sentence is either true or false. If we say that, however, then we deliberately forget about the fact that some statements such as e.g. "books smell blue", "the king of America is tall", $\sqrt{-1} < 2$ or $a[10] < a[11]$ in the context of a declaration **integer array** $a[0..10]$, are simply senseless.

Two—valued mathematical logic has emerged as a theory of mathematical proofs. Since the latter are sequences of formulas which must be permanently valid in their domains of interpretation, senseless formulas cannot appear in proofs and therefore they have been expelled from the theory. Of course, in constructing a proof (i.e. in proving a theorem) we may come across a potentially senseless formula, such as e.g. $\sqrt{x}<2$ or a[i]<a[i+1]. Such a case, however, is regarded as an error in reasoning, and is usually repaired by "strengthening the assumptions", i.e. by restricting the domain where formulas are expected to be valid. Of course, a proof—reparation step of that sort is not expressible in the classical proof theory. On the ground of two—valued logic, senseless formulas belong to the world of "non—formulated operativeness".

The game which we play with proofs cannot be repeated when we use predicates in algorithms, e.g. in programs or in the denotational specifications of software. In that case predicates do not represent statements which express some general laws, but tests which are "dynamically" performed in order to select an appropriate branch of an algorithm. The partiality of these predicates may have different sources. It may result from the "physical" bounds of machine arithmetic as in

$$y < x + z$$

or from the use of mappings (e.g. arrays) as data types, as in

$$a[i] < a[i+1]$$

or from the fact that the evaluation of some functions (procedures) may lead to nonterminating computations, as in

$$FAC.x > x^2$$

where $FAC.x = x=0 \rightarrow 1, x*FAC.(x-1)$.

Partial predicates cannot be avoided in algorithms. On the other hand, any attempt to the evaluation of a predicate in the domain of its undefinedness leads to a failure. In order to avoid such situations we must be able to describe and analyze them, and this requires the introduction of partial predicates to our formalism.

For technical convenience, instead of investigating partial predicates with two possible values tt and ff, we shall investigate total predicates with three values tt, ff, and ee (error). As we shall see later, ee in our model may be interpreted either as an error signal which results from abortion, or as a true undefinedness which results from a nonterminating computation.

In order to distinguish between classical and non—classical truth values we introduce two domains:

    Bool   = {tt,ff}
    Boolerr = {tt,ff,ee}

The elements of the former will be referred to as **classical boolean values** and those of the latter as **pseudo—boolean values**.

Predicates are usually constructed on the ground of the calculus of functions (Sec.Sec.4 and 5) in using logical operators such as propositional connectives **and, or, not**, etc. and quantifiers. Of course, all logical operators must be extended to the three—valued case.

Let us start from propositional connectives, which in our case are total functions from Boolerr to Boolerr. It is rather obvious that for classical arguments tt and ff the extended connectives must give the same values as in the classical case. The problem is how to define them for ee.

A possible — and apparently a very natural — solution is to agree that all new connectives are **strict**, i.e. assume a value ee whenever at least one of their arguments is ee. That solution, although widely accepted in the intuitive treatment of undefinedness, is rather inconvenient for our applications. To see that consider the following example.

Assume that we have defined two predicates p:A→Boolerr and q:B→Boolerr where A and B are disjoint domains and that we want to define a third predicate r:A|B→Boolerr which tests the property expressed by p in A and the property expressed by q in B. Such a situation appears frequently in applications, e.g. when we use a case constructor.

Our new predicate may be easily defined on the ground of the calculus of functions by the equation r = p|q. This, however, is a rather inconvenient solution. When we compose predicates from other predicates we prefer to use propositional connectives. In the first attempt to define r in that way we may try to write the following equation:

r.x = if xεA **then** p.x **fi and**
     if xεB **then** q.x **fi**   (9.1)

where "=" denotes the equality in Boolerr and where **if—then—fi** and **and** denote the usual implication and conjunction. Unfortunately, this is an incorrect solution. Observe that if our propositional connectives are strict, then r.x=ee for all xεA|B since for any x in A|B either p.x=ee or q.x=ee. It is easy to show, that in using strict propositional connectives one cannot define r as a propositional combination of p and q.

Strictness of abstract functions corresponds to a so called **eager evaluation** of expressions. When we "eagerly" evaluate **if** xεA **then** p.x **fi** then we first evaluate both subexpressions xεA and p.x and only when this step is completed we compute the final value of implication. Of course, if xεA evaluates to ff, then p.x is undefined and therefore the whole computation fails.

An alternative to eager evaluation is **lazy evaluation**. Informally speaking when we lazily evaluate an expression we only evaluate "as many of its argument subexpressions as it is necessary to establish the value of the whole expression". For instance, in our case we first evaluate xεA and if this yields ff, then we abandon the evaluation of p.x and we assume that the implication yields tt, since according to a classical principle "if false **then** something" should always be true.

Mathematically, the lazy evaluation of implication leads to the following non-strictness property of **if—then—fi**:

if ff **then** bb **fi** = tt   for any bb ε Boolerr

As is easy to check, if we assume that property, then (9.1) becomes equivalent to the equation r = p|q.

The principle of lazy evaluation may be also applied to other three-valued propositional connectives. Consider another example, this time from the field of imperative programming:

```
integer array a[1..10];
i:=1;
while i<10 and a[i] < a[i+1]
    do i:=i+1 od
```

That program is supposed to find the index of the first element of an array which is not smaller than its successor element. Of course, if **and** is strict, i.e. if **and** is evaluated eagerly, then our program will abort for every array which is ordered increasingly. However, if similarly to implication we assume the following non-strictness of conjunction:

ff **and** bb = ff   for any bb ε Boolerr

then **and** may be evaluated lazily in which case our program will always terminate properly.

Below we describe a propositional calculus with three-valued non-strict propositional connectives. That calculus was proposed by John McCarthy [McCarthy 1961] and will serve us as a starting point for the construction of a calculus of three-valued predicates. We start from the definition of McCarthy's conditional operator:

−Mc→ : Boolerr x Boolerr x Boolerr → Boolerr

For any a,b,c ε Boolerr,

a −Mc→ b, c =
        a=tt → b,
        a=ff → c,
        a=ee → ee

Using that operator we now define McCarthy's propositional connectives. For any a,b ε Boolerr:

not a	= a −Mc→ ff, tt	**negation,**
a **or** b	= a −Mc→ tt, b	**alternative,**
a **and** b	= a −Mc→ b, ff	**conjunction,**
if a **then** b **fi**	= a −Mc→ b, tt	**implication.**

Beside that we define

a iff b = if a **then** b **fi and if** b **then** a **fi**

and for **if** a **then** b **fi** we assume an alternative notation:

a **implies** b.

McCarthy's connectives have four important properties:

1) They are direct extensions of classical connectives, i.e. are
identical to them when restricted to Bool = {tt,ff}.

2) They allow for a lazy evaluation (except for **not** which has
only one argument) and in that case they again coincide with
classical operators.

3) They are monotone in a flat cpo over Boolerr (Fig.9.1), i.e.
if in

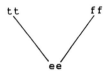

Fig.9.1

a propositional expression we replace one of its current arguments
by ee, then the value of that expression either remains unchanged,
or becomes ee.

4) They are strict with respect to left argument, i.e. assume
value ee whenever their left argument is ee.

Due to these properties McCarthy's connectives may be understood as
classical connectives lazily-evaluated in a three-valued environment.
Observe also that property 4) allows us for the implementation of our
calculus even if ee denotes an unrepairable failure, such as e.g.
nontermination.

Now we proceed to the calculus of predicates. In order to describe it
in a simple and sufficiently systematic way we shall assume that
predicates are functions on states, where states are mappings from
some identifiers to some values:

Predicate = State → Boolerr
State   = Ide $\xrightarrow{m}$ Value

Our treatment of predicates is half way between the style of mathematical logic, where one introduces a formalized language of terms and formulas, and a pure functional-calculus. In the former style, one has to deal with many technicalities which we do not want to talk about at this moment. In the latter, there is no way to define quantifiers. Our approach allows us for the introduction of quantifiers without introducing a formalized language.

In our calculus of predicates we use the following predicate constructors:

$$\textbf{\underline{not}} : \text{Predicate} \to \text{Predicate}$$
$$\textbf{\underline{and}, \underline{or}, \underline{implies}} : \text{Predicate} \times \text{Predicate} \to \text{Predicate}$$
$$\forall : \text{Ide} \to \text{Predicate} \to \text{Predicate}$$
$$\exists : \text{Ide} \to \text{Predicate} \to \text{Predicate}$$

The first four correspond in an obvious way to propositional connectives. For instance **and** is defined by means of **and** in the following way:

$$(p \ \textbf{\underline{and}} \ q).sta = p.sta \ \textbf{and} \ q.sta$$

for any p,q∈Predicate and any sta∈State. In a similar way we define **not**, **or** and **implies**. Instead of the latter we also write **if then fi**. By tt, ff and ee we denote predicates which assume values tt, ff and ee respectively, for any state.

Now let us define quantifiers. For every p∈Predicate, every ide∈Ide and every sta∈State we set:

∀.ide.p.sta = tt if for any value val∈Value, p.sta[val/ide] = tt;

ff if there exists a value val∈Value such that p.sta[val/ide] = ff;

ee otherwise, i.e. if for no val∈Value, p.sta[val/ide] = ff, but there exists a val such that p.sta[val/ide] = ee.

∃.ide.p.sta = tt   if there exists a value val∊Value such that p.sta[val/ide] = tt;

        ff if for any value val∊Value, p.sta[val/ide] = ff;

        ee otherwise, i.e. if for no val∊Value, p.sta[val/ide] = tt, but there exists a val such that p.sta[val/ide] = ee.

As is easy to check, all our predicate constructors — including quantifiers — coincide with the corresponding classical constructors on the domain of classical predicates, i.e. predicates with only two values. This leads to many similarities between our calculus and the classical one. Of course, there are also several differences. In order to discuss and prove the properties of our calculus we introduce a set-theoretic representation of three-valued predicates. Our construction is analogous to the representation of classical predicates on the ground of a boolean algebra of sets. With every predicate p we associate two sets of states:

$$T.p = \{sta \mid p.sta=tt \}$$
$$F.p = \{sta \mid p.sta=ff \}$$

which we call respectively the **positive characteristic set** and the **negative characteristic set** of p. As is easy so see, these sets characterize p unambiguously, i.e. for any two predicates p and q,

$$T.p = T.q \text{ and } F.p = F.q \quad \text{iff} \quad p = q$$

In the classical case we have, of course,

$$T.p = State - F.p$$

and therefore we need only one of these sets in order to characterize a predicate.

Below we list equations which show how to calculate the characteristic sets of compound predicates when we have such sets for their components. As we shall see later, these equations are very helpful in proving several properties of our predicate constructors.

1) T.(**not** p)   = F.p

   F.(**not** p)   = T.p

2) T.(p **or** q)   = T.p | (F.p n T.q)

   F.(p **or** q)   = F.p n F.q

3) T.(p **and** q)   = T.p n T.q

   F.(p **and** q)   = F.p | (T.p n F.q)   (9.2)

4) T.(p **implies** q)   = F.p | (T.p n T.q)

   F.(p **implies** q)   = T.p n F.q

5) T.[∀.ide.p]   = $\bigcap_{val \varepsilon Value}$ {sta | sta[val/ide]εT.p}

   F.[∀.ide.p]   = $\bigcup_{val \varepsilon Value}$ {sta | sta[val/ide]εF.p}

6) T.[∃.ide.p]   = $\bigcup_{val \varepsilon Value}$ {sta | sta[val/ide]εT.p}

   F.[∃.ide.p]   = $\bigcap_{val \varepsilon Value}$ {sta | sta[val/ide]εF.p}

Predicates are used in denotational semantics in the construction of functions and domains, and in the description of certain properties of software systems (Sec.10). In all these applications it is important to know when one predicate may be replaced by another without altering the meaning of the construct where it appears. In order to describe appropriate rules, and also in order to formulate some general laws of our calculus, we define four relations between predicates:

≡, <=>,   ⊑, => : Predicate x Predicate → Bool

We call these relations **superpredicates** since they may be regarded as predicates on predicates. Note that superpredicates are two-valued. Let p,q ε Predicate:

p and q are **strongly equivalent**, in symbols

    p ≡ q

if T.p = T.q and F.p = F.q, i.e. if p and q are equal as functions. We use "≡" to denote the equality of predicates in order to distinguish that equality from the equality of values which we denote by "=".

p and q are **weakly equivalent**, in symbols

    p <=> q

if T.p = T.q, i.e. if p.sta=tt implies q.sta=tt and vice versa.

p is **less defined than** q, in symbols

    p ⊆ q

if T.p ⊆ T.q and F.p ⊆ F.q, i.e. if p.sta=tt implies q.sta=tt and p.sta=ff implies q.sta=ff. Observe that "⊆" is a vertical ordering induced in Predicate by the flat ordering of Fig.9.1 in Bollerr.

p is **stronger than** q, in symbols

    p => q

if T.p ⊆ T.q, i.e. if p.sta=tt implies q.sta=tt.

Observe that in the classical case ≡, <=> and ⊆ coincide. In the three-valued case they are, however, different. Consider the following examples:

    1) x>0 **and** √x>2 ≡ x>4

    2) √x>2 <=> x>4 but neither "≡" nor " " hold

    3) √x<2 ⊆ x<4 but neither "≡" nor "<=>" hold

    4) x>4 => x>3 but neither "⊆" nor "<=>" hold

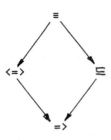

Fig.9.2

As is easy to see "≡" is the strongest of our four relations and

"=>" is the weakest. Two remaining are mutually independent. This is shown on Fig.9.2 where downward arrows denote set—theoretic inclusion.

Both "≡" and "<=>" are, of course, equivalence relations in the domain of predicates. However, whereas the former is obviously a congruence (Sec.3) with respect to all predicate constructors, the latter enjoys this property only with respect to **and** and both quantifiers, i.e. p<=>p′ and q<=>q′ imply:

$$p \text{ \textbf{and} } q \quad <=> \quad p′ \text{ \textbf{and} } q′$$
$$(\forall \text{ide})p \quad <=> \quad (\forall \text{ide})p′$$
$$(\exists \text{ide})p \quad <=> \quad (\exists \text{ide})p′$$

An easy proof follows from (9.2). It is also easy to check that similar properties do not hold for other connectives. In particular, p<=>p′ does not imply **not** p <=> **not** p′. For instance, $\sqrt{x}>2$ <=> x>4 is true, but $\sqrt{x} \leqslant 2$ <=> x $\leqslant$ 4 is not.

From the viewpoint of applications our superpredicates may be split into two groups: ≡ and ⊑ in one and <=> and => in the other. The former come into play whenever we use predicates in the construction of functions or algorithms, e.g. in denotational semantics or in programming. In these cases whenever we replace a predicate by another one we must observe either strong equivalence, in which case we do not change the meaning of the whole construct where it appears, or we only make sure that the new predicate is better defined than the former, in which case our new function (or algorithm) has a not smaller domain of definedness. For instance, in a command:

1) **while** x>4 **do** ...

we may replace x>4 by x>0 **and** $\sqrt{x}>2$ getting

2) **while** x>0 **and** $\sqrt{x}>2$ **do** ...

but we cannot replace it by $\sqrt{x}>2$ since in that case the new program

3) **while** $\sqrt{x}>2$ **do** ...

aborts for all x<0, whereas 1) and 2) only exit the loop in that case. On the other hand, if we replace $\sqrt{x}>2$ in 3) by $x>4$, then the new program terminates (with the same result) wherever the old does.

Strong equivalence need not be observed if we use predicates to represent sets. Typical applications are well—formedness conditions for domains or pre— and post—conditions in correctness statements (Sec.10). In all these cases a predicate p represents only the set T.p and therefore all modifications of the definition of p may be performed up to weak equivalence. For instance:

$$\{x \mid \sqrt{x}>2\} = \{x \mid x>4\}.$$

Similarly, if we want to restrict or enlarge a defined set we take a stronger, or respectively a weaker predicate.

Below we list some major laws of our calculus. All of them may be proved by simple set—theoretic reasoning on the ground of (9.2). We first list these properties which hold also in the classical case. Later we show differences. Let p,q,r ε Predicate:

1) **and** and **or** are associative,

2) **and** is left distributive over **or** and vice versa,

3) usual de Morgan's laws hold between **not**, **and** and **or**,

4) p **and** p ≡ p,

   p **or** p ≡ p,

5) p **or** (p **and** q) ≡ p,

   p **and** (p **or** q) ≡ p,

6) **not** (**not** p) ≡ p,

7) p **or** ff ≡ p

   ff **or** p ≡ p,

8) p **and** tt ≡ p

   tt **and** p ≡ p,

9) p => p **or** q,

   p **and** q => p,

10) **not** (∀ide)p ≡ (∃ide) **not** p,

   not (∃ide)p ≡ (∀ide) **not** p,

The most significant differences between the classical— and the three-valued calculus of predicates are the following:

11) **and** is not right distributive over **or** and vice versa,

12) **and** and **or** are not commutative, and moreover

    a) p **and** q <=> q **and** p, i.e. **and** is weakly commutative,

    b) **or** is not even weakly commutative,

13) p **or** **not** p ⊑ tt, but "≡" does not hold,

    p **and** **not** p ⊑ ff, but "≡" does not hold,

14) (∀ide)p **and** (∀ide)q <=> (∀ide)(p **and** q), but "≡" does

                                           not hold

    (∀ide)p **and** (∀ide)q ⊑ (∀ide)(p **and** q),

15) (∃ide)p **or** (∃ide)q ⊑ (∃ide)(p **or** q), but "<=>" does

                                           not hold

To make the discussion of our calculus complete we should identify and explain the relationship between two different conceptual levels which we have dealt with: the **object level** and the **metalevel**.

The **object level** is the level of denotational definitions of software. At that level we <u>use</u> three-valued predicates in order to describe the behavior of software systems. Operations **not**, **or**, **and**, etc., constants tt, ff and ee, relations, operations and constants of data-types such as e.g. <, + or ↑ all belong to that conceptual level. The notation which we introduce at that level provides a starting point for a future development of a formalized language of denotational definitions.

The **metalevel** is the level where we <u>talk about</u> three-valued predicates and their calculus. Operations **not**, **or**, **and**, etc., constants **tt**, **ff** and **ee**, relations ≡, <=>, ⊑, => and finally the constructors of functions and relations all belong to that metalevel. The notation which we introduce at that level will not appear in our future language of denotational definitions. It may, however, appear in the definition of that language.

An explanation should also be given to the way in which we have introduced quantifiers. Formally, we have defined them at the metalevel, since only at that level we have formally introduced identifiers. It is quite clear, however, that we need quantifiers at the object level as well. Since a formal introduction of quantifiers at that level requires a formalization of the metalanguage – which would go beyond the scope of this book – we introduce them only informally as a certain notation. We assume that whenever we write a predicative formula preceded by a quantifier, we denote in that way a predicate which results in the application of the corresponding quantification operation to the predicate denoted by that formula.

The difference between our two conceptual levels may be better explained if we explicitly show the types of functions which belong to different levels. Let us take three of them as an example:

implies : Boolerr x Boolerr → Boolerr

implies : Predicate x Predicate → Predicate

=>   : Predicate x Predicate → Bool

Observe that the range of => is Bool rather than Boolerr. At the metalevel we use classical two-valued logic, since at that level we only _talk_ about algorithms rather than _construct_ them. Propositional connectives of that level are (not underlined thinface) "not", "and", "or", "iff", etc. and are not formalized.

On the classical ground we frequently forget about the difference between the mentioned levels since for two-valued predicates:

$$p \Rightarrow q \quad \text{iff} \quad p \ \underline{\textbf{implies}} \ q \equiv tt \tag{9.3}$$

and (p **implies** q) ≡ tt iff p.sta **implies** q.sta = tt for any sta. In the intuitive reasoning based on the two-valued logic we do not care too much whether we say that "x>4 is stronger than x>2" or that "x>4 implies x>2".

It should be emphasized that (9.3) does not hold in the three-valued case. In that case we only have two following (meta) implications:

p **implies** q ≡ tt   implies   p => q

p => q   implies   p **implies** q ⊑ tt

None of the converse implications hold. The counterexamples are the following:

[p **and** q] => [q **and** p]

is true for all p and q since **and** is weakly commutative, but [(p **and** q) **implies** (q **and** p)] ≡ tt

does not hold, e.g. if p ≡ **ee**. Similarly

    [(p **or** q) **implies** (q **or** p)] ⊑ tt

is true for all p and q, but

    [p **or** q] => [q **or** p]

does not need to hold since **or** is not weakly commutative.

It may be worth mentioning that (9.3) is true whenever p is a total
predicate, i.e. whenever

    (p **or** **not** p) ≡ tt

This fact   is of a paramount importance when one develops a
three-valued logic. In this section, however, we do not discuss this
subject. Our calculus has been fully defined on the ground of set
theory and therefore we can use two-valued logic in proving facts
about our three-valued predicates. We can also use three-valued
predicates to express the properties of some data types (models). In
that case, however, we have to remember that our calculus offers us
two different types of theorems which we may formulate about data
types. We may formulate **strong theorems** which say that a given
property p is always true:

    p ≡ tt

or **weak theorems** which say that a given property   p is never
false:

    p ⊑ tt

For instance, in the usual arithmetic of reals

    x<4 **implies** √x<2

is a weak theorem, whereas

$(x>0$ **and** $x<4)$ **implies** $\sqrt{x}<2$

is a strong theorem.

Besides the usual "logical" properties of the calculus of three-valued predicates, which we have discussed above, we may also be interested in the continuity properties of our predicate constructors, since in denotational definitions some predicates may be defined by fixed-point equations. Observe that since Boolerr constitutes a flat cpo (Fig.9.1), the set Predicate with the corresponding vertical ordering is a cpo as well. Now it is easy to prove that all our predicate constructors, including

∃.ide, ∀.ide : Predicate → Predicate

are continuous. This proof is left to the reader.

At the end of this section some remarks are in order about two different approaches to the problem of using three-valued predicates in applications.

At the first place we should mention an approach which is known from mathematical logic and which consists in axiomatizing a semantic consequence relation based on the calculus of three-valued predicates, i.e. in developing a nonclassical deduction system. Since the early paper of J.Łukasiewicz [Łukasiewicz 20], several such systems have been developed on the ground of general mathematics (see [Rasiowa 74] and references there) and also in the context of computer science (see [Hoogewijs 79,83,87] and [Barringer,Chang,Jones 84]. As turns out in all these cases the three-valued deduction systems are substantially different from the classical one. To use them requires a technical familiarity with mathematical logic and an ability of carrying out formalized — in contrast to just formal — proofs. In such proofs one cannot rely on the usual (two-valued) intuitions, since several classical laws do not hold.

In **MetaSoft**, hence also in this book, we assume an alternative approach which consists in regarding three-valued predicates, along with the calculus of relations, functions, domains, etc., as one of the calculi defined and used on the ground of set-theory and the classical two-valued logic. Due to the introduction of superpredicates, which are two-valued, we can use three-valued predicates in expressing on the ground of classical logic all facts about data and algorithms which we can express on the ground of a formalized three-valued logic. In fact, using superpredicates we can say even more, since "=>" is not expressible by propositional connectives. In Sec.10 we show how to construct program-correctness proof-rules in terms of superpredicates. It should also be mentioned that the proofs of facts expressed by three-valued predicates and two-valued superpredicates may be supported by classical theorem-proovers or proof-checkers. For instance, a proof-checker MIZAR (see [Marciszewski 87] for a general description and references) has been expanded by our predicate calculus and used as a computer tool in proving such facts in connection with program development by transformations [Woronowicz 86].

INPUT—OUTPUT CORRECTNESS STATEMENTS

When we design a software product — whether this is a simple program, a programming language or a complex integrated system — we may wish to specify some of its expected properties and to verify later if they are satisfied. If they are, then we say that our software is **correct** with respect to these properties. Statements which express such properties are therefore called **correctness statements**.

When software is developed in accordance with the principle of structured programming, then large software components are combined from smaller ones — called modules — by means of some standard operations. For instance, when we are programming in Pascal, then modules may correspond to expressions, commands and declarations, and operations may correspond to ":=", ";", <u>if</u> <u>then</u> <u>else</u>, etc. Now, if we want to prove the correctness of our software the most rational way to do this is to use so called **structural induction**, i.e. to carry out proofs by induction on the structural complexity of modules. In that case, in turn, it is convenient to have for every module constructor

$$f : A_1 \times \ldots \times A_n \to B$$

a lemma of the form:

    if modules $a_1, \ldots, a_n$ satisfy a condition p,
    then (or then and only then)   (10.1)
    module $f.\langle a_1, \ldots, a_n \rangle$ satisfies a condition q .

A collection of such lemmas may be regarded (and used) as a proof system, where our lemmas play the role of proof rules. Precisely speaking a formalized proof system may be derived from such lemmas.

A proof system derived in the described way is always **sound**, i.e. guarantees that in using it one shall never prove a false theorem. At the same time, however, it is in general not complete, i.e. not every true fact may be proved in it. The incompleteness of software—oriented proof systems is the consequence of the incompleteness of practically all (second order) formalized theories. The latter has been known from the famous works of a German mathematician Kurt Goedel (see e.g. [Kleene 52]).

The general mathematical infeasibility of the construction of a complete proof system for software neither means that we can never construct a practically usable systems nor that in such a construction we may forget about the issue of completeness because our systems must be incomplete anyway.

The general mathematical incompleteness of formalized theories is a deep metamathematical fact which, however, does not affect too much the life of a "working mathematician". True but unprovable statements which may be constructed on the ground of second order theories are highly artificial and one can hardly expect them to appear in practice. On the other hand, when we construct a proof system we should make sure that it is not "more incomplete than unavoidable", i.e. that we have not forgotten about some necessary rules and/or that our rules are not too weak. More formally, we must be aware of two sources of conceptual errors which may lead to a "practical incompleteness" of our system:

1) There may be no lemmas in the system for some of our module constructors in which case we may be unable to prove anything about modules which have been build in using these constructors. The first requirement for a practical completeness of a system is, therefore, that the system must contain a proof—rule for every constructor.

2) Our lemmas may be too weak i.e. their premises may be too strong. We may be unable to use a lemma in the proof of a true fact because its premise is too strong. The second requirement for a practical completeness of a proof system is, therefore, that all — or at least as many as possible — of our proof—rules have the if—and—only—if form.

In general, when we are establishing a specialized proof system where the properties of software are expressed in a language which extends the usual language of logic (we shall see such a system later in this section), then we regard such a proof system as sufficiently complete if — simplifying a little — its proof rules allow for the reduction of every special statement about the correctness of software to a usual logical statement. In that case we say that our system is **relatively complete**, by which we mean that its incompleteness is due to only the unavoidable general incompleteness of formalized theories.

Now, when we have discussed the issue of completeness, let us make a few remarks about who and when may use a software—correctness proof system. In fact, there are two principal conceptual levels at which such a system can be used.

First, we may have such a system at the level of a metalanguage of software specification. At that level the system serves a software designer in proving specific properties of his software and in deriving a lower level proof rules for the benefit of the user of that software. E.g. if the concerned software is a programming language, then its designer may wish to prove that no command or declaration destroys the well—formedness of states, that assignments and "read"—commands have a certain effect, that objects declared in a block are not visible outside of that block, etc. When this is done the designer will develop proof rules for a lower—level proof system of the user of the language.

At that lower level the user of the language will use the formerly developed proof rules to proof some specific properties of concrete programs. E.g. he will prove that a program A properly sorts every input file and never goes into a loop and that a program B correctly prepares a sorted file for a printer. In his proofs he will apply proof—rules developed by language designer, some general facts about the system (as mentioned above), also established by the designer and some general mathematical facts about data types of the program.

It should be mentioned in this place that the lower—level proof system does not necessarily need to be developed after the software itself has been denotationally specified. In some situations a proof system for a future software can make part of its nonalgorithmic predenotational specification.

In this section we shall not deal with a proof system of any specific level. We shall show some general rules which can be used in establishing proof systems of both levels. On the other hand, we shall restrict our attention to a special type of software properties called **input—output** **correctness** (abbreviated I–O correctness). These properties have been investigated since long on the ground of Floyd—Hoare theory of program correctness and are adequate for deterministic software modules and also, to a limited extend, in the description of some local properties of concurrent systems. According to the principle assumed in this book, we shall not develop a formalized proof system based on a formalized language, but we shall show lemmas of the form (10.1) from which formalized inference rules may be derived when necessary.

Since input—output properties concern the transition of some inputs into some outputs, we shall discuss them on the ground of the algebra of binary relations (Sec.3). For a technical convenience we restrict ourselves to relations where the left domain and the right domain is the same. We denote this domain by State and therefore we assume that all our relations belong to the set Rel.<State,State>. We assume nothing about the domain State besides that it is not empty. Let RεRel.<State,State> and p,q:State→Boolerr.

We say that R is **partially correct** with respect to precondition p and postcondition q, in symbols

$$\textbf{prtpre } p : R \textbf{ prtpost } q \qquad\qquad (10.2)$$

if

$$(T.p)R \subseteq T.q$$

i.e. if for every input state which satisfies p every corresponding output state satisfies q. Putting this in different words, we require that whenever we "execute" R with an input state which satisfies p and whenever this execution terminates successfully (i.e. neither aborts nor goes into an infinite loop), then the output state satisfies q.

Partial—correctness statements may be used to describe properties of nondeterministic systems which run permanently. Assume for example that we are designing an operating system which has n actions

$R_1, \ldots, R_n$ in its repertoire. Assume further that each of R_i's may be chosen by a signal from an external environment, but since we do not want to model that environment as a part of our system, we regard each choice of R_i as nondeterministic. We assume that after having performed an action our system becomes ready to perform any other action and so on. Now, we may wish to claim (and prove) that if we initialize the system with a state which satisfies p, then at any moment when the system completes the execution or R_i, the state will have a property q_i. Formally we can express our conjunction as the following partial-correctness statement:

prtpre p : $(R_1 | \ldots | R_n)^{\ulcorner *} R_i$ **prtpost** q_i

As we said, partial correctness does not guarantee termination. A property which does guarantee termination is total correctness. We say that R is **totally correct** with respect to a precondition p and a postcondition q, in symbols:

totpre p : R **totpost** q

if

$T.p \subseteq R(T.q)$

i.e. if for every input state which satisfies p, there exists a corresponding output state which satisfies q. Observe that total correctness does not guarantee that any execution of R which starts in T.p will terminate successfully in T.q. If R is not a function, then there may be many executions of R which start from the same initial state in T.p and such that one of them does not terminate properly (i.e. aborts), another does not terminate at all, and yet another terminates outside of T.q. Total correctness only says that at least one execution from T.p will correctly terminate in T.q. For nondeterministic systems total correctness is a relatively weak property. In fact, however, it is most frequently applied to deterministic programs. In that case the existence of a correct output simply means that the unique output exists and is correct.

Readers familiar with [Manna,Pnueli 74] approach to total correctness should note that our total correctness is different from the former. In the Manna and Pnueli case R is always a function and is called totally correct wrt   p   and   q   if it is partially correct with respect to p and q and if every execution which starts from p is finite. This finiteness does not exclude abortion, i.e. a so called non—clean termination is allowed. Our total correctness is sometimes called **clean total correctness** [Blikle 81a].

Now, we shall discuss some basic techniques of proving partial— and total—correctness of abstract binary relations. Precisely speaking we shall show how to reduce the correctness problem for a relation composed from other relations by relational constructors to a similar correctness problem for component relations. We shall investigate relational composition, union, conditional union (generalized in an obvious way to relations) and an arbitrary fixed—point constructor. Since lemmas which we are going to show may be used as partial— and total—correctness proof rules, we shall express them in a notation typical for inference rules in logic. We shall use diagrams:

```
    X                    X
   ---       and        ===
    Y                    Y
```

which we read as   "if Y then X"   and   "X if and only if Y" respectively. Formulas   X   and Y will be (possibly quantified) conjunctions of some subformulas. In that case commas which separate these formulas stand for   "and". Let us   start from partial correctness. By P,Q,R,... we denote relations and by   p,q,r,... we denote predicates. PC stands for "partial correctness".

(PC—1)

> **prtpre** p : PQ **prtpost** q
> =============================
> there exists r   such that
> 1) **prtpre** p : P **prtpost** r,
> 2) **prtpre** r : Q **prtpost** q

Proof. If part: If   (T.p)P $\subseteq$ T.r and (T.r)Q $\subseteq$ T.q, then by the monotonicity of the composition of a set with a relation we have ((T.p)P)Q $\subseteq$ T.q and by the restricted associativity property of that operation we have   (T.p)(PQ) $\subseteq$ T.q. Only if part: take any r such that T.r = (T.p)P. For this r, 1) and 2) obviously hold.   □

(PC-2)

    prtpre p : P|Q **prtpost** q

    ==============================

    1) **prtpre** p : P **prtpost** q

    2) **prtpre** p : Q **prtpost** q

Proof is obvious by the distributivity of the composition of a set
and a relation over a union of relations.

(PC-3)

    prtpre p : **IF** s **THEN** R **ELSE** Q **FI** **prtpost** q

    ==

    1) **prtpre** (p **and** s) : R **prtpost** q

    2) **prtpre** (p **and** **not** s) : Q **prtpost** q

<u>Proof</u>. From (PC-2) by three following observations:

    (i)   **IF** s **THEN** R **ELSE** Q **FI** = (id.(T.s))R | (id.(F.s))Q

    (ii) (T.p)[id.(T.s))R] = [T.(p **and** s)]R

    (iii) (T.p)[id.(F.s))Q] = [T.(p **and** **not** s)]Q

(PC-4) Let R be the least solution of a fixed-point equation
X = F.X, where F is a continuous function on relations:

    prtpre p: R **prtpost** q

    ==

    prtpre p : $F^i.\phi$ **prtpost** q   for all i ⩾ 1

Proof follows immediately from Klenee's theorem (Thm.2.1) and the
distributivity of composition over unions.

The last lemma is of little practical value. Of course, as long as we
know nothing about F, we cannot expect too much from the
corresponding proof rule. If, however, F is specific and
sufficiently simple, then one may usually come up with a much more
"practical" rule. For instance, if F.X = P | QX, i.e. if R is the
least solution of X = P | QX, then we have the following:

(PC-4.1)

    prtpre p : R **prtpost** q
    ==============================
    there exists r such that:
    1) p => r
    2) **prtpre** r : Q **prtpost** r   (r is called an **invariant** of Q)
    3) **prtpre** r : P **prtpost** q

<u>Proof</u>. If part: From 2) one may prove by a simple induction that for any $n>0$, $(T.r)Q^{rn} \subseteq T.r$. Therefore, by 1) and 3), $(T.p)Q^{r*}P \subseteq T.q$. But $Q^{r*}P$ is the least solution of our equation. Only if part: Show that any r such that $T.r = (T.p)Q^{r*}P$ satisfies 1), 2) and 3).

Proof rules which we have formulated so far correspond to basic constructors of relations. To these rules we add one which allows for the   strengthening   of   preconditions and the weakening   of postconditions. Note that this is only an "if" rule:

(PC-5)

    prtpre p_1 : R **prtpost** q_1
    ----
    prtpre p : R **prtpost** q, p_1 => p, q => q_1

Proof is obvious.

Observe now that the "if" parts of our lemmas (i.e. the bottom-up implications) guarantee the soundness of the corresponding proof rules, whereas the "only if" parts guarantee their relative completeness. In this particular case the relative completeness means that any true correctness statement of the form:

    prtpre p : R **prtpost** q

may be proved provided that:

    1) we are able to express in our language all necessary intermediate predicates r which appear in the proof,
    2) we are able to prove - on the ground of the underlying

formalized mathematical theory of our data types — all formulas of the form $p \Rightarrow r$, $p_1 \Rightarrow p$ and $q \Rightarrow q_1$ which appear in the proof,

3) we are able to prove all intermediate correctness statements which appear in the proof and which concern nondecomposable relations, i.e. relations defined in some other way than as a combination of other relations.

When we construct a partial—correctness proof system for a concrete specification metalanguage or for a concrete software, then we can usually provide sufficiently many proof—rules to make the completeness of our system not relative to 3). However, as follows from our former remarks, we can never make it fully complete, i.e. not relative to 1) and 2).

Now let us proceed to total correctness. As we shall see similar lemmas may be proved in that case as well.

(TC-1)

    totpre p : PQ **totpost** q

    ================================

    there exists r such that:
    1) **totpre** p : P **totpost** r,
    2) **totpre** r : Q **totpost** q

Proof analogous to that of (PC-1).

(TC-2)

    totpre p : P|Q **totpost** q

    ======================================

    there exists r_P and r_Q such that:
    1) $p \Rightarrow r_P$ **or** r_Q,
    2) **totpre** r_P : P **totpost** q,
    3) **totpre** r_Q : Q **totpost** q

<u>Proof</u>. If part: Simple calculations which refer to monotonicity and distributivity of composition. Only if part: Choose any r_P and r_Q such that $T.r_P = P(T.q)$ and $T.r_Q = Q(T.q)$.

(TC-3)

> **totpre** p : **IF** s **THEN** P **ELSE** Q **FI totpost** q
> ==
> 1) p => s <u>or</u> <u>not</u> s
> 2) **totpre** (p <u>and</u> s) : P **totpost** q,
> 3) **totpre** (p <u>and</u> <u>not</u> s) : P **totpost** q

Proof similar to that of (PC-3). Note that 1) says the following: if p is satisfied, then s is defined.

(TC-4) Let R be the least solution of a fixed-point equation X = F.X, where F is continuous.

> **totpre** p : R **totpost** q
> ==
> there exists an infinite sequence of predicates
> $r_1, r_2, \ldots$ such that:
> 1) p => r_1 <u>or</u> r_2 <u>or</u> ...
> 2) **totpre** r_i : $F^{r_i}.\phi$ **totpost** q   for all i=1,2,...

<u>Proof</u>. Define r_1 <u>or</u> r_2 <u>or</u>... as the (unique) predicate which corresponds to the following pair of characteristic sets (see Sec.9): $(U_{i=1}^{\infty} T.r_i, \bigcap_{i=1} F.r_i)$. The rest of the proof is similar to that of (PC-4).

Similarly as for (PC-4) also in this case we can derive a "more practical" rule if R is the least solution of X = P | QX:

(TC-4.1)

> **totpre** p : R **totpost** q
> ==
> there exists an infinite sequence of predicates $r_1, r_2, \ldots$
> such that:
> 1) p => r_1 <u>or</u> r_2 <u>or</u> ...
> 2) **totpre** r_i : Q **totpost** r_{i-1} for all i=2,3,...
> 3) **totpre** r_1 : P **totpost** q

<u>Proof</u>. If part: similar to that of (PC-4.1). Only if part: Choose r_i such that $T.r_i = (Q^{r(i-1)}P)(T.q)$.

(TC-5)

    totpre p : R **totpost** q, p_1 => p, q => q_1

----

    totpre p_1 : R **totpost** q_1

Proof is obvious.

All remarks about the consistency and the relative completeness of the proof system for partial correctness apply in this case as well.

BIBLIOGRAPHIC REMARKS

Sec.2 contains a collection of rather obvious and widely known consequences of ideas described in [Kleene 52] and [Tarski 55]. Therefore no particular references may be given to the theorems of that section. The idea that fixed point techniques may be used in defining the denotations of programs was for the first time suggested in an unpublished paper [Scott,de Bakker 69], but the first paper which gives a mathematical justification of that fact and proves the equivalence of a fixed-point and an operational semantics is [Mazurkiewicz 70]. The use of fixed-point equations in the semantics of programs was then further investigated in the 1970'ties by many authors of which to mention only the earliest (in an alphabetic order) are [de Bakker 71], [Blikle 71], [Park 70], [Scott 70], [Scott,Strachey 71].

The calculus of binary relations described in Sec.3 bases mainly on the early papers of the author and of A.Mazurkiewicz [Blikle 71, 72] [Blikle,Mazurkiewicz 72], [Mazurkiewicz 72] where binary relations were used as a general framework for an operational and a fixed-point semantics of programs. That calculus was later extended, generalized and further applied in [Mazurkiewicz 73] and [Blikle 74, 77, 77a, 77b]. A slightly different version of that calculus was also used by J.de Bakker and his followers, see [de Bakker 80] and references there.

The calculus of functions described in Sec.4 and Sec.5 is only a slight modification and a formalization of that calculus used in VDM [Bjørner,Jones 78, 82]. In an earlier and a less complete version it was also formalized in [Blikle 83].

Sec.6 covers only very simple technicalities and therefore there are no references to it.

Sec.7 gives a very preliminary information about an algebra and a cpo of formal languages. An advisable further reading on that subject may be [Harrison 78]. More information about the definability of context-free languages by fixed-point equations may be found in [Blikle 72a].

The calculus of domains described in Sec.8 has been originally published in [Blikle,Tarlecki 83] along with a discussion about its applicability to denotational semantics.

Sec.9 is devoted to the discussion of a three-valued predicate calculus. The more general issue of a three-valued logic is as old as the pioneer paper by a Polish logician and philosopher (the author of a so called Polish notation) Jan Łukasiewicz [Łukasiewicz 20]. In contrast to our calculus his propositional connectives are not monotone, e.g. in his case

(ee **implies** ee) = tt

The non-monotonicity of propositional calculus destroys the recursiveness of predicates. For that reason eighteen years later S.C.Kleene [Kleene 38] (see also [Kleene 52]) described another three-valued calculus where all operators are monotone. That calculus was later investigated in [Hoogewijs 79, 83] and in [Barringer, Cheng,Jones 84] from the viewpoint of its applications in the theoretical computer science. In contrast to our case, Kleene's **and** and **or** are commutative. This gives the calculus more regularity, but at the same time, due to its non-strictness, requires unbounded parallelism for implementation. Technically this follows from the fact that in Kleene's case

(ee **or** tt) = (tt **or** ee) = tt

In 1961 John McCarthy suggested in [McCarthy 61] a propositional calculus where **and** and **or** are not commutative and therefore, although not strict, can be implemented sequentially. At the same time, however, McCarthy has introduced nonmonotone (noncontinuous) quantifiers. In our calculus we have used McCarthy's propositional connectives and generalized classical quantifiers which are continuous. That calculus was applied earlier by the author in the context of an abortion-free correctness of programs [Blikle 81a] and programs' systematic development by transformations [Blikle 78, 81].

Sec.10 is devoted to a model—theoretic description of an axiomatic approach to program correctness which is due to C.A.R.Hoare [Hoare 69]. Actually Hoare's original paper dealt with partial correctness only. Total correctness was described and formalized later by [Manna, Pnueli 74] in a way which did not exclude abortion. An abortion—free total correctness, so called clean total correctness, was discussed on a model—theoretic ground in several papers: [Blikle,Mazurkiewicz 72], [Hitchcock,Park 72], [Mazurkiewicz 73], [Blikle 77b, 81a] and references in the latter. All these approaches have a common root known as the assertion method of proving the correctness of programs. That method in known due to the work of R.W.Floyd [Floyd 67]. It should be mentioned here that for the first time assertion method, including total correctness, was published as early an in 1949 by Alen Turing [Turing 49]. Unfortunately it has not been appreciated by the contemporary and remained unknown for several years.

EXERCISES

All exercises are numbered by pairs of integers of which the first indicates the number of the corresponding section. (*) marks more difficult exercises.

2.1 Prove that $(A \not\Rightarrow B, \subseteq)$ is a cpo. Show an example of such a subset F of $A \not\Rightarrow B$ for which F does not exist.

2.2 Show that the least element of a set is always the unique minimal element of that set byt not vice versa.

2.3 Prove that the operations on cpo's defined in Sec.2 really lead from cpo's to cpo's.

2.4 Prove that every continuous function is monotone.

3.1 Prove that the operation of the composition of relations is associative, distributive over unions and monotone.

3.2 Prove that the operations of the power and of both iterations of relations are continuous.

3.3 Prove that any two equivalence classes of an equivalence relation are either equal or disjoint.

4.1 Prove that the horizontal and the vertical ordering of functions are cpo orderings.

4.2 Prove the continuity in respective variables of the conditional union, overwriting and restriction in the cpo of partial functions.

4.3 (*) Prove that if C ranges over a cpo of sets which are ordered by inclusion but where lub's are not unions, and if f ranges over partial functions, then f\C need not be continuous in C.

4.4 Prove that in the cpo $(A \rightarrow B, \sqsubseteq)$ of total functions with vertical ordering the composition of functions is not continuous in the first argument.

4.5 Prove that in the cpo $(A \rightarrow B, \sqsubseteq)$ of total functions with vertical ordering the conditional union **IF p THEN f ELSE g FI** is continuous in p:$A \rightarrow B$ if B is a flat cpo.

4.6 (*) Construct a non-flat cpo for which the function of 3.5 is not continuous in p and another one for which it is continuous. Find a weaker condition for B than flatness which still guarantees the continuity of the conditional union in p.

4.7 (*) The same as 4.3 but for total function.

Sec.Sec. 5 and 6 introduce essentially only some notation and therefore no exercises to them may be thought.

7.1 Prove that the operations of concatenation, power, and both finitistic iterations of languages are continuous in the cpo of formal languages.

7.2 (**) By a **polynomial** over a subset Bas of a cpo of formal languages we mean any function on languages which may be constructed in composing constant functions with values in Bas, concatenation and union. E.g. F.X = A, F.X = X, F.⟨X,Y,Z⟩ = AXBYXZCDY where A,B,C,D∈Bas are examples of polynomials over Bas. Now prove the following (cf.[Blikle 72a]):

7.2.1 For any fixed alphabet Alf, if Fil denotes the class of all finite languages over Alf, then the set of all languages definable by polynomial fixed-point equations over Fil is equal to the set of all context-free languages over Alf.

7.2.2 The same (i.e. 7.2.1) holds true if we enrich the set of equations by admitting both plus- and star- iterations.

7.2.3 The same (i.e. 7.2.1 and 7.2.2) holds true if we enrich the class Fil by admitting all regular languages or even all context-free languages.

7.3 (*) Prove that both infinitary iterations on generalized languages are not continuous in the corresponding cpo.

8.1 Prove the continuity of continuous operations on domains.

8.2 (*) Prove the noncontinuity of the noncontinuous operations on domains. Prove that some of these operations are monotone (which?).

8.3 (*) Define an algorithm which checks whether a given (finite) set of domain equations is legal in the sense that all noncontinuous functions which appear in it are not used in recursive definitions of domains.

9.1 Prove the properties 1)-14) of three-valued predicates. Hint: use equations 9.2.

10.1 Give full formal proofs of all PC and TC proof rules.

P A R T   T W O

AN EXAMPLE DEFINITION
OF A SUBSET OF PASCAL

Sec. 1

INTRODUCTION

Our example is devoted to a formal analysis of the mechanisms of records and pointers in Pascal. For the sake of this analysis we define a subset of Pascal which contains these mechanisms. In order to make our discussion possibly short and clear we restrict standard types to only integers and booleans and structured types to records without variants. We also drastically restrict the classes of expressions and commands leaving only a necessary minimum which we need for the discussion of type-correctness issue. We totally omit procedures, blocks and goto's since these mechanisms were discussed in [Blikle, Tarlecki 83]. We also omit input-output commands since their definitions are quite straightforward. In this and in the subsequent sections we frequently refer to the original report on Pascal [Jensen, Wirth 78] which we call REPORT and to the ISO standard of Pascal in [Wilson, Addyman 82] which we call STANDARD.

Our prime concern is to give a precise and a possibly abstract definition of Pascal types. That concept, although of paramount importance for the language, has not been given a satisfactory definition neither in REPORT nor in STANDARD. The former gives a very inadequate definition, the latter does not give any and does not even

list the concept of a type in the Index. At the same time both REPORT
and STANDARD frequently refer to that concept, e.g. in the
explanation of type—compatibility rules for assignment and for
procedure calls.

The lack of a precise definition of a type in Pascal leads to many
ambiguities. Consider as an example the following fragment of a
Pascal program and try to analyze the relationship between the types
which appear there:

```
type                                              (1.1)
    number = integer;
    size   = number;
    item   = record x:number; y:size end;
    object = record x:number; y:size end;
    parcel = object;


var                                               (1.2)
    i    : integer;
    n    : number
    it   : item;
    re₁  : record x:integer; y:integer end;
    re₂  : record x:integer; y:integer end;
```

In order to carry out such analysis we have to find out what REPORT
and STANDARD say about the concept of a type. In REPORT we find the
following explanation:

> "A data type determines a set of values which variables of that
> type may assume and associates an identifier with that type."

This definition is not very satisfactory. First of all, it does not
say what a type is, but only what it "determines". Second, it refers
to the concept of a value, which is nowhere defined in the REPORT.
Third, it is not very adequate. Indeed. if in this definition we
assume that "determines" means "is" and that a value in Pascal is any
mathematical entity which may be assigned to a variable, then we must
come to the following conclusion about our types:

1) *integer, number* and *size* denote equal types,
2) *item, object* and *parcel* denote equal types,

3) variables re_1 and re_2 are of the type denoted by *item*.

Of course, only the first of these sentences will be satisfied in a typical Pascal implementation. The second and the third will not. This means that REPORT's definition of a type does not match the common understanding of that concept. Not only that *item* and *object* denote different types, the anonymous types of re_1 and re_2 have no identifiers associated to them.

STANDARD tries to be closer to the reality about types (Sec.Sec. 6.4.5, 6.4.6, 6.4.7), but at the same time it is even less precise than REPORT, since it does not define the concept of a type at all. Instead it introduces a syntactic notion of a **new-type** and distinguishes between type definitions which refer to previously defined types, like:

    size = number;

and these which introduce a new type explicitly like:

    item = **record** x:number; y:size **end**;

In the latter the right-hand side of the definition is referred to as a **new type**.

The introduced syntactic classification serves in the following semantic (?) rule about types (Sec.6.4.1 of STANDARD):

Each occurrence of a **new-type** shall denote a type that is distinct from any other **new-type**.

On the base of that rule we can conclude that *item* and *object* denote different types. Further conclusions may be only guessed and here two different interpretations of the rule are possible. One may either assume that whatever has not been said in STANDARD has been left open, or one may assume that STANDARD explains only unclear points about Pascal and remains tacit about everything which is commonly known.

The first interpretation is equivalent to admitting that STANDARD's semantics is ambiguous. The second, that it is readable only for those who already know Pascal. In each case one has to agree that STANDARD does not provide a complete, self-contained and unambiguous definition of Pascal types.

For the sake of our definition of Pascal types we shall assume the second interpretation. This leads to the following equivalence classes between the types of (1.1) and (1.2):

1) {*integer, number, size*},
2) {*item*},
3) {*object, parcel*},
4) {the anonymous type of re_1},
5) {the anonymous type of re_2},

The major source of ambiguity and confusion about types in programming languages (where Pascal provides only one example) comes from the fact that the syntax and the semantics of types are conceptually mixed together and that the word "type" is used very ambiguously to mean many different things. In order to avoid all these ambiguities in our definition we formally introduce five following concepts:

1) **type**; and a **named type** as a subcase,
2) **type carrier**: a set of objects of a given type,
3) **type identifier**: an identifier whose value is a type,
4) **type expression**: an expression whose value is a type,
5) **type definition**: a statement which assigns a type to a type identifier.

For instance:

item = **record** x:number, y:size **end**

is a type definition. The right-hand side of that definition is a type expression. A type expression in not yet a type. The latter may be computed as a value of a type expression in a given **static environment**. In our case the type which is assigned to the **type identifier** *item* in the context of (1.1), belongs to the class of so called **record types** and formally is a mapping:

[(integer)/x, (integer)/y]

where "(integer)" denotes a type permanently assigned to the reserved type identifier "integer". A type cannot be identified with a set of values, since two different types may correspond to the same set of values. An example of such a situation comes later in this section. Intuitively (integer) may be understood as a machine name of a set of integers.

The elaboration of a type definition results in the association of a type to a type identifier. A snapshot of an assignment between identifiers and types is called a **static environment**. For instance, the elaboration of (1.1) generates the following static environment:

$$
\begin{aligned}
&\text{number} \rightarrow \text{(integer)} &&(1.3)\\
&\text{size} \quad \rightarrow \text{(integer)}\\
&\text{item} \quad \rightarrow \langle\text{item, [(integer)/x, (integer)/y]}\rangle\\
&\text{object} \rightarrow \langle\text{object, [(integer)/x, (integer)/y]}\rangle\\
&\text{parcel} \rightarrow \langle\text{object, [(integer)/x, (integer)/y]}\rangle
\end{aligned}
$$

Types assigned to type identifiers "item", "object" and "parcel" belong to the class of so called **named types**. Each of these types is an ordered pair which consists of an identifier (name) and a type. This allows for the distinction between the types assigned to "item" and "object" thus fulfilling the guessed interpretation of the STANDARD's rule.

The elaboration of the declarations of variables assigns types marked by a label "mk-var-descr" to variable identifiers. The labeling serves the purpose of distinguishing — at the level of static environment — between type identifiers and variable identifiers of a given type. For instance, the elaboration of (1.2) in the environment (1.3) extends the latter by the following assignments:

$$
\begin{aligned}
&\text{i} \quad \rightarrow \text{mk-var-descr((integer))}\\
&\text{n} \quad \rightarrow \text{mk-var-descr((integer))}\\
&\text{it} \quad \rightarrow \text{mk-var-descr(}\langle\text{item, [(integer)/x, (integer)/y]}\rangle\\
&\text{re}_1 \rightarrow \text{mk-var-descr(}\langle\text{re}_1\text{, [(integer)/x, (integer)/y]}\rangle\\
&\text{re}_2 \rightarrow \text{mk-var-descr(}\langle\text{re}_2\text{, [(integer)/x, (integer)/y]}\rangle
\end{aligned}
$$

Each type identifies a set of values called a **type carrier**. The carrier of (integer) is the set Int of all machine representable integers. The types assigned in (1.3) to "item", "object" and "parcel" have the same common carrier:

$$\{[loc_1/x, loc_2] \mid loc_i \; \varepsilon \; Loc\}$$

where Loc denotes the set of all memory locations.

The reader may wonder why the elements of this carrier are mappings from identifiers to locations rather than from identifiers to integers. The choice of a location-oriented model of records has been forced by the fact that in Pascal an expression like

    item.x

may denote either a value or a location. It denotes a value on the right-hand side of an assignment and on the position of an actual value-parameter of a procedure. It denotes a location on the left-hand side of an assignment and on the position of an actual reference-parameter of a procedure. We shall return to this issue later.

Of course, in the semantics of Pascal we have to describe also the assignment of values to identifiers. For that purpose we introduce **dynamic environments** which map identifiers to locations, and **stores**, which map locations to values. Further we define a **state** as a triple which consists of a static environment, a dynamic environment and a store. An expression like item.x may be evaluated in a given state either by a so called **left-hand-side semantics** in which case the value of the expression is a location, or by a **right-hand-side semantics** in which case this value is an integer.

AN INFORMAL DESCRIPTION OF OUR SUBSET OF PASCAL

Our subset has two standard data types, **boolean** and **integer**, and two classes of user-definable data types, **records** and **pointers**.

Every identifier in a program is either a **type identifier** or a **variable identifier**. A type identifier must be declared by a **type definition** and serves later in the program as an identification of the defined type. Every type definition, except from a pointer-type definition, must refer only to the previously defined types. A pointer-type definition may refer to a (yet) undefined type. Of course, in a complete program all types which are referred to must be defined.

A **variable identifier** must be declared by a **variable declaration** which binds to it a type description and a memory space. A variable declaration does not assign any value to a variable and therefore any right-hand-side reference to a variable in a program must be preceded by an initialization of that variable. No identifier may be declared twice in one program, but every identifier used in a program must be declared in it.

Expressions in our language belong to two (syntactically not disjoint) classes of **left expression** and **right expressions**. A left expression is either an **identifier** or a **field designator** or a **dereference expression**. A right expression is either an **arithmetic expression** or a Boolean expression.

Simple commands are restricted to **assignments**, **new pointer generations** and **pointer disposals**. Structured commands are constructed by means of ";", **if_then_else_fi** and **while_do_od**.

Each program consists of a possibly empty sequence of type definitions, followed by a nonempty sequence of variable declarations, followed by a nonempty sequence of commands.

ABSTRACT SYNTAX

The concept of abstract syntax, first described in [McCarthy 61] and
[Landin 64] and later formalized in [Goguen, Thatcher, Wagner, Wright
77], has been introduced in order to distinguish between the
structure and the spelling of the syntax of a programming language.
For instance the following three different syntactic forms of a
conditional command:

$$\text{if exp } \textbf{then } com_1 \textbf{ else } com_2 \textbf{ fi} \qquad\qquad (3.1)$$
$$\textbf{case exp true } com_1 \textbf{ false } com_2 \textbf{ end}$$
$$\textbf{IF } exp \rightarrow com_1 \mid com_2 \textbf{ FI}$$

may be regarded as having a common structure expressible in the form
of the triple:

$$(exp, com_1, com_2) \qquad\qquad (3.2)$$

We say that (3.2) is a common **abstract syntax** of all of (3.1),
whereas each of (3.1) provides a different **concrete syntax** for
(3.2).

If Exp, Com and Con-com denote the syntactic domains of expressions,
commands and conditional commands, then a concrete syntax definition
which corresponds to the first case in (3.1) is:

$$\text{Cond-com} = \{if\}^\wedge Exp^\wedge \{then\}^\wedge Com^\wedge \{else\}^\wedge Com^\wedge \{fi\}$$

whereas the corresponding equation in the abstract-syntax definition
is:

$$\text{Cond-com} = Exp \times Com \times Com$$

In the definitions of abstract syntax we frequently use labeled
domains (cf. Sec.8 in Part One). For instance, we may define the

abstract—syntax domain for conditional commands as follows:

    Cond—com :: Exp x Com x Com

In that case the elements of Cond—com are of the form:

    mk—cond—com(exp, com$_1$, com$_2$)

This style contributes to the redundancy of abstract syntax thus making it more readable. The same technique may be used in distinguishing between two abstract—syntactic concepts which have the same structure but different semantics. For instance, the abstract syntax of "**goto** ide" command is simply "ide" (the identifier), but since identifiers and **goto**—commands have obviously different meanings, they must also have different abstract syntaxes. We shall write therefore:

    Ide   = ...
    Goto :: Ide

When we define a denotational semantics of an existing programming language it is convenient to start from the definition of its abstract syntax since it is usually a few times shorter than the definition of the corresponding concrete syntax, c.f. a formal definition of Ada [Bjørner, Oest 80] and a formal definition of full Pascal [Andrews, Henhapl 82].

Below we define the abstract syntax of our subset of Pascal. We use the domain constructors and the notation introduced in Sec.6 and Sec.8 of Part One.

Program

    Program   = Type-def-part x Var-dec-part x Com

Type definition

    t—def   : Type-def   = {<>} | Ide x Type-exp |
                              Type-def x Type-def
    t—exp   : Type-exp   = Type-name | Rec-t-exp | Point-t-exp
    t—name   : Type-name   = Stand-t-name | Ide

```
                Stand-t-name    = {boolean} | {integer}
    ide      : Ide             = (identifiers; a predefined domain)
    r-t-exp  : Rec-t-exp       = Var-dec-part
    p-t-exp  : Point-t-exp     :: Type-name
```

Variable declaration

```
    v-dec    : Var-dec    = Ide^{c+} x Type-exp |
                            Var-dec x Var-dec
```

Expression

```
    exp      : Exp        = Left-exp | Right-exp
    l-exp    : Left-exp   = Ide | Field | Deref
    field    : Field      = Left-exp x Ide
               Deref      :: Left-exp
    r-exp    : Right-exp  = Arit-exp | Bool-exp
    a-exp    : Arit-exp   = {one} | Left-exp | Plus-exp
               Plus-exp   :: Arit-exp x Arit-exp
    b-exp    : Bool-exp   = {true} | Left-exp | And-exp
               And-exp    :: Bool-exp x Bool-exp
```

Command

```
    com      : Command   = Assign | New | Dispose | If | While |
                           Com x Com
               Dispose   :: Left-exp
               Assign    :: Left-exp x Right-exp | Left-exp x {nil}
               New       :: Left-exp
               If        :: Boll-exp x Com x Com
               While     :: Boll-exp x Com
```

Note 1 We assume that "boolean", "integer", "one", "nil" and "true"
do not belong to Ide.

Note 2 Record-type expressions, which constitute the domain
Rec-t-exp have been defined as variable declaration parts. This has a
very natural explanation: each record defines a block of local
variables.

SEMANTIC DOMAINS

By **semantic domains** in a denotational definition of a language we traditionally mean the domains of denotations, the domain of states and all other domains which appear in the definitions of the former, such as e.g. the domains of environments, of stores, of types, of location, of values etc.

In our semantic model of Pascal we assume that each state has three components: a **static environment**, a **dynamic environment** and a **store**. We therefore define:

    sta : State = Stat-env x Dyn-env x Store

Static environment records this information about identifiers which is used in compile-time, i.e. in the static processing of a program. Dynamic environments and stores record all the remaining information.

It should be emphasized that in our definition we do not distinguish between so called **static semantics** and **dynamic semantics** (cf. [Andrews, Henhapl 82]). Such a distinction although certainly quite convenient for compiler designers, does not contribute to the readability of a definition. Our definition is user-oriented and has been written in the style of a one-pass abstract interpreter.

4.1 STATIC DOMAINS

The class of static domains contains static environments and all semantic domains used in the definition of the former.

Static environment

    s-env   : Stat-env = Ide $\underset{m}{\rightarrow}$ Ide-descr
             Ide-descr = Type-descr | Var-descr | {EXPECTED}

Type

```
t-descr   : Type-descr        = Type
type      : Type              = Standard-type | Named-type
            Standard-type     = {(boolean),(integer)}
            Named-type        = Ide x Non-standard-type
            Non-standard-type = Record-type | Pointer-type
            Record-type       = Ide ⇥ Var-descr
                                     m
            Pointer-type      :: Domain-name
d-name    : Domain-name       = Standard-type | Ide
```

Variable description

```
v-descr   : Var-descr         :: Type
```

Static environment associates type descriptions or EXPECTED to type
identifiers and variable descriptions to variable identifiers. The
reserved symbol EXPECTED is assigned to an identifier whenever we
elaborate a pointer-type declaration where this identifier is a
domain name which has not been defined yet as a type (Sec.6.3).

A **type description** is simply a type. A **type** is either a standard
type or a named type. The latter is a non-standard type preceded by
an identifier (see Sec.1 for explanation).

A **variable description** is a type labeled by a mark indicating that
the associated identifier is a variable. Formally, every variable
description is of the form mk-var-descr(type), where type∈Type.

4.2 DYNAMIC DOMAINS

The class of dynamic domains contains the domains of dynamic
environments, of stores and all other semantic domains which appear
in their definitions.

Dynamic environment

```
d-env     : Dyn-env = Ide ⇥ Loc
                           m
```

```
    loc        : Loc      = (locations; a predefined set)
```

Store

```
    sto        : Store       = Loc ⇀ Pseudo-value
                                   m
    p-val      : Pseudo-value = Value | {RESERVED}
```

Value

```
    val        : Value = Boll | Int | Rec | Loc | {NIL}
    b          : Bool  = {(true),(false)}
    i          : Int   = {i | m⩽i⩽M, i∊Integer}  ;  m<M
    rec        : Rec   = Ide ⇀ Loc
                             m
```

Dynamic environments bind locations to identifiers. **Stores** bind pseudo-values to locations. A **pseudo-value** is either a value or a reserved symbol RESERVED. The latter is used at a stage of variable declaration (Sec.6.4), where we only allocate store without initializing a variable with any value. Locations in the domain of values represent pointers. The domain Integer denotes a predefined set of all integers.

4.3 THE ALGEBRA OF DATA

Essentially the algebra of data should have been defined prior to dynamic domains since the domains of data appear in the definitions of dynamic environment and store. In Pascal, however, the usual hierarchy of concepts is partially destroyed by the use of locations (in records and pointers) as values. Since the concept of a location can be explained only in the context of dynamic environments and stores, it seem justified to talk about Pascal data after having introduced dynamic domains.

Our many-sorted algebra [Goguen et.al. 77] of data contains six carriers:

```
    Ide, Bool, Int, Rec, Loc, {NIL}
```

which were defined in the former section, and five operations on these carriers:

```
(true)  :  → Boll
and     :  Boll x Bool → Boll
1       :  → Int
plus    :  Int x Int → Int|{ERROR}
select  :  Rec x Ide → Loc|{ERROR}
```

The zero—argument operations "(true)" and "1" represent reserved constants. The remaining operations have obvious definitions which we omit. We only assume that "plus" and "select" may generate error messages. For "plus" this is an overflow signal. Function "select" signalizes an error whenever the selecting identifier does not belong to the domain of the record.

Due to the special Pascal requirement about records (cf. Sec.1) which forces us to define records as mappings from identifiers to locations rather than from identifiers to values, we get a mathematical model of a record which is rather far from a typical Pascal—user intuition. Indeed, in this model (i.e. without referring to the concept of a store) we cannot say anything about the possible values of field variables. We cannot say that these values may be booleans, integers, records or pointers. We cannot explain the possibility of constructing circular structures using records with pointers. We cannot even define the operation of updating records since an assignment to a record field, such as:

```
re.x := a—exp
```

modifies a store rather than a record!

As we shall see later all mentioned mechanisms and attributes associated to records may be described at a level where we can talk about stores (Sec.6). This is, of course, not the level of a data—type algebra, but of machine—memory model. The fact that records in Pascal cannot be regarded as "pure data", such as e.g. integers, is the consequence of the location—oriented model of records, which in turn is the consequence of having reference (rather than value—result) parameters in procedures (cf. Sec.1).

The fact that our model of records is rather far from the common intuition of Pascal users' only means that this intuition is far from the literal Pascal meaning of records. Pascal is much more machine- and implementation-oriented than it is commonly thought.

WELL—FORMED STATES

The domain of states, which we have defined so far, is too large in the sense that besides correct Pascal states it contains also states which shall never appear the executions of programs. It is so because in the definition of the domain State we have assumed nothing about the relationship between the defined types, the types of declared variables and the values of these variables.

The mentioned situation is not restricted to the case of states. All domains which appear in the definitions of software are in general larger than their subsets effectively "reachable" by implementations. For instance, syntactic domains contain only context—free oversets of context—sensitive formal languages of expressions, declarations, commands, programs, etc. The corresponding domains of denotations usually contain all partial or total functions between some domains of states and/or values, rather than only these functions which are the denotations of syntactic objects.

Domain equations only exhibit a general structure of each domain thus helping the author (and the reader) of software definition in constructing the definitions of functions on these domains — such as semantic functions, denotations, etc. — and in avoiding typing errors. The effectively "reachable" subsets of these domains are in general defined only implicitly. For instance, well—formed programs are defined by static error—generation mechanism.

In the case of states we usually define the reachable subset explicitly since the understanding of properties which generable states must satisfy is paramount for the further understanding of other mechanisms of the language. In particular, it is necessary for a correct formulation of the semantics of expressions, declarations and commands as well as for the derivation of program—correcness proof rules. In this section we define predicates which explicitly identify the set of states reachable by program executions.

5.1 AUXILIARY FUNCTIONS

Here we define a few auxiliary functions which are used   later in this
and in the following sections.

   new : Integer $\not\to$ Store $\to$ Loc^{c+}

   $(\forall n \geqslant 1)(\forall sto)(new.n.sto = (loc_1,...,loc_n)$ where
   $(\forall 1 \leqslant i,j \leqslant n)(\text{if } i \neq j \text{ then } loc_i \neq loc_j \text{ fi}$
                   $\text{and } loc_i \notin dom.sto)$

This function when given a positive integer n and a store   sto
returns n (fresh) locations which are   not bound in sto. We use this
function to model the memory allocation mechanism.

   demark

This is a generic function which remover a mark from an arbitrary
marked object. For instance: demark.mk−point−t−exp(d−name) = d−name.

   domain−types : Type $\to$ Ide−**finset**

   domain−types.(boolean) $= \{\}$
   domain−types.(integer) $= \{\}$
   domain−types.mk−pointer−type((boolean)) $= \{\}$
   domain−types.mk−pointer−type((integer)) $= \{\}$
   domain−types.mk−pointer−type(ide) $= \{ide\}$
   domain−types.$[type_1/ide_1,...,type_n/ide_n] =$
                             $U_{i=1}^n domain\text{−}types.type_i$
   domain−type.$\langle ide,type \rangle$ $= domain\text{−}types.type$

The value of that function for the argument "type" is the set of all
identifiers which appear in that type as the names of domain−types of
pointer types.

   types : Static−env $\to$ Ide−**finset**

```
types.s-env = {ide | s-env.ide ε Type}
```

The value of that function in a given static environment is the set
of all identifiers which have been defined as types.

```
variables : Static-env → Ide-finset

variables.s-env = {ide | s-env.ide ε Var-descr}
```

The value of that function in a given static environment is the set
of all identifiers which have been declared as variables.

```
remove-name : Type → Type

remove-name.type =
    type ∉ Named-type → type
    let <ide,type₁> = type in
    TRUE              → type₁
```

This function removes the name from any named type and passes every
unnamed type unmodified.

```
field-ide : Var-dec → Ide-finset

field-ide.<<ide₁,...,ideₙ>,t-exp> = {ide₁,...,ideₙ}
```

This function creates the set of all identifiers which appear in a
variable declaration. This is to be used in Sec.6.2.

5.2 WELL-FORMEDNESS PREDICATES

In this section we define the property of a well-formedness of a
state. The semantics of our subset of Pascal is then defined in such
a way that all type definitions, variable declarations and commands
preserve that property of states.

Since the well-formedness property establishes the relationship
between the static environment, the dynamic environment and the store

of a state it is expressed in the form of a predicate on states. We shall construct that predicate in a top—down manner.

All predicates defined in this section are formally regarded as functions with values in the three element set

Bollerr = {tt,ff,ee}

which has been introduced in Sec.9 of Part One. In their definitions we use three—valued propositional connectives and quantifiers which were also discussed in that section. The definitions of our predicates are written in the style of the definitions of functions with formal parameters (Sec.5 of Part One). The definitional equality which appears there is the identity in the domain Boolerr.

well—formed—state : State → Boolerr

well—formed—state.<s—env,d—env,sto> =
   well—defined—types.s—env **and**
   well—typed—variables.s—env **and**
   well—allocated—variables.<s—env,d—env,sto>

We start from the well—definedness of types which again has a top—down definition.

well—defined—types : Stat—env → Boolerr

well—defined—types.s—env =
   well—described—types.s—env **and**
   no—types—expected.s—env

The two component predicates are defined as follows:

well—described—types : Stat—env → Boollerr

well—described—types.s—env =
   $(\forall ide \in types.s-env)(\forall ide_1 \in domain-types.(s-env.ide))$
     $(s-env.ide_1 \ \varepsilon \ Type|EXPECTED)$

Types are well described if all identifiers which denote domain types are either defined as types or are bound to EXPECTED.

```
no-types-expected : Stat-env → Boolerr
```

```
no-types-expected.s-env = (∀ide)(s-env.ide ≠ EXPECTED)
```

Types are well defined if every identifier which appears in a type as a domain-type identifier is also bound to some type. Observe that this property does not exclude the circularity of types, but such a circularity — as we shall see in Sec.6.3 — is only possible via pointer types.

Now we proceed to properties which concern variables. The fist is of a static character:

```
well-typed-variables : Stat-env → Boolerr
```

```
well-typed-variables.s-env =
    (∀ideεvariables.s-env)
        (domain-types.(demark.(s-env.ide)) ⊆ types.s-env)
```

Variables are well typed if every identifier declared as a variable is associated to a type where all domain types have been previously defined.

The second variable-oriented property of states describes the correspondence between the declared type of a variable, the memory allocated to that variable and the content of that memory:

```
well-allocated-variable : State → Boolerr
```

```
well-allocated-variable.<s-env,d-env,sto> =
    (∀ideεvariables.s-env)
        d-env.ide ε Loc and
        let loc=d-env.ide in
        let type=demark.(s-env.ide) in
        well-filled.<loc,type,s-env,sto>
```

Variables are well allocated if every identifier declared as a variable is bound in the dynamic environment to a location and if this location is well-filled in the store with respect to the declared type of the variable taken in the context of the current static environment. The latter context is necessary in order to evaluate the possible occurrences of domain-type identifiers in the type of the variable. Below we define the well-filledness property. The definition is, of course, recursive:

```
well-filled : Loc x Type x Stat-env x Store → Boolerr

well-filled.<loc,type,s-env,sto> =
    loc ε dom.sto                                          and
    let p-val=sto.loc in
    if type=(boolean) then p-valεBool|{RESERVED} fi and
    if type=(integer) then p-valεInt|{RESERVED} fi   and
    if typeεRecord-type
        then
            let
                [v-descr₁/ide₁,...,v-descrₙ/ideₙ]=type
            in
            let
                typeᵢ=demark.v-descrᵢ for i=1,...,n
            in
            (∃loc₁,...,locₙ)
                ([loc₁/ide₁,...,locₙ/ideₙ]=p-val and
                (∀1≤i≤n)(well-filled.<locᵢ,typeᵢ,s-env,sto>))
    fi                                                     and
    if typeεPointer-type
        then
            p-valε(Loc|{NIL}|{RESERVED}) fi        and
            if p-valεLoc
                then
                    let d-name=demark.type in
                    if d-nameεStandard-type
                        then well-filled.<p-val,d-name,s-env,sto>
                    fi
                    if d-name∉Standard-type
                        then d-nameεtypes.s-env and
                            let d-type=s-env.d-name in
                    well-filled.<p-val,d-type,s-env,sto[RESERVED/loc]
                    fi
            fi
    fi
    if typeεNamed-type
        then
```

```
        let <ide,type₁>=type in
        well-filled.<loc,type₁,s-env,sto>
    fi
```

This definition requires a more detailed explanation. Informally, we can read it as follows: If "type" is a standard type, then loc must be filled either with an appropriate standard value or with RESERVED. If "type" is a record type, then loc must be filled with an appropriate record whose field-locations must be well-filled accordingly to the types of the corresponding field identifiers. If "type" is a pointer type, then loc must be filled either with another location or with NIL, or with RESERVED. In the former case we have to check, if this another location — which in our definition is denoted by p-val — is well-filled. If our pointer type has a standard domain type, then p-val must be well-filled accordingly to that standard type. If, however, it points to an identifier which is a name of another type — we denote it by d-name — then we cannot simply check the well-filledness of p-val with respect to d-type since p-val may be a node in a circular structure in which case our induction would "never terminate". In order to avoid such a situation we cut the potential loop at its very beginning in assigning to loc the pseudovalue RESERVED. As is easy to check, the cut loop is well-formed if and only if the original loop was well-formed. Here is an example. Consider the following declaration:

```
type
    link = ↑ring;
    ring = record y:integer; z:link end
var
    x:link
```

and the following dynamic environment and store:

$$x \to loc_1 \to loc_2$$
$$loc_2 \to [loc_3/y, loc_1/z]$$
$$loc_3 \to 2$$

In order to check the well-filledness of loc_1 with respect to the type "link" in that store we check the well-filledness of loc_2 with respect to the type "ring" in the following modified store:

$x \rightarrow loc_1 \rightarrow$ RESERVED

$\qquad loc_2 \rightarrow [loc_3/y, \ loc_1/z]$

$\qquad loc_3 \rightarrow 2$

In this new store the loop associated to loc_1 has been cut.

One more remark is in order about the definition of the "well-filled" predicate. It should be noticed that this definition is correct only under the assumption that our propositional connective **if_ then fi** is McCarthy's implication as defined in Sec.9 of Part One. Indeed, in several **if_then_fi** clauses, e.g. in

$\qquad$ **if** type ε Pointer-type **then** ... **fi**

when the premise is false, the conclusion has an undefined value.

DENOTATIONS

In this section we describe the denotations of all syntactic objects of our language. For that sake we first introduce the concept of an **abstract error** [Goguen 77]. Intuitively an abstract error represents an error message which is generated by the implementation of the language whenever the execution of a program must be aborted. Formally this is a distinguished element ERROR which becomes the value of a function of denotation when the arguments of that function do not satisfy certain conditions.

Let for every domain Dom:

$$Dom^E = Dom \mid \{ERROR\}$$

The **semantic functions** of our language, i.e. functions which assign denotations to syntax, are of the following types:

P	: Program	→ State	⇸	State^E
TE	: Type-exp	→ Stat-env	→ Type^E	
TD	: Type-def-part	→ Stat-env^E	→ Stat-env^E	
VD	: Var-dec-part	→ State^E	→ State^E	
L	: Left-exp	→ State	→ Type^E × Loc^E	
R	: Right-exp	→ State	→ Type^E × Value^E	
C	: Com	→ State^E	⇸	State^E

We assume that an error message corresponds to a detectable (i.e. a computable) erroneous situation such as a type error, an overflow error, an index error, etc. The generation of an error is equivalent to abortion: it terminates the execution of a program and cannot be called off. This is mathematically modeled by assuming that the denotations of type definitions, variable declarations and commands may accept ERROR as an argument and in this case return ERROR as a value. We say that these functions are **error preserving**. Intuitively speaking, whenever ERROR is generated somewhere in the program it is then passed unchanged by the remaining part of the program and becomes the output of the program in the place of a final state.

Our model of the error elaboration mechanism is rather simplified: First, we assume to have only one abstract error, which means that we identify all possible causes of an error. Second, we assume that the generation of an error in program execution is unreparable. Both these simplifications are only technical and have been adopted for the simplicity of our example. What is relevant in our model is that ERROR represents a "computable undefinedness", i.e. that it appears as a value of a function if and only if one may effectively decide that the actual argument of that function does not belong to the domain of that function. If, however, the value of a function for a given argument cannot be computed because this involves an infinite computation process (a loop), we assume that the value of the function for this argument is undefined. This is why the denotations of programs and commands are partial functions.

In the subsections which follow we define our semantic functions. We assume that metavariables which range over domains Dom^E are the same as metavariables which range over the corresponding Dom. For instance, sta now ranges over $State^E$, s-env now ranges over $Stat\text{-}env^E$, etc.

6.1 PROGRAMS

The denotation of a program is a partial function which transforms a state into another state or into ERROR:

P : Program $\rightarrow$ State $\leftrightarrow$ State^E

$P[\langle t\text{-}def,v\text{-}dec,com\rangle].\langle s\text{-}env,d\text{-}env,sto\rangle =$
    let s-env$_1$ = TD[t-def].[] **in**
    s-env'=ERROR $\rightarrow$ ERROR,
    not no-types-expected.s-env$_1$ $\rightarrow$ ERROR,
    TRUE $\rightarrow$ (VD[v-dec]•C[com]).$\langle$s-env',[],[]$\rangle$

The transformation of a state by a program is effectuated in the following way: First the definitions of types are elaborated in an empty static environment thus creating a new static environment s-env'.If in this elaboration process an error message is generated, then program execution is aborted and this message is returned in the place of the output state of the program. Otherwise we check if all types which are referred to in type definitions have been defined. If this is not the case, then an error message is generated and the execution aborts. Otherwise the created static environment with the empty dynamic environment and the empty store are passed to variable declarations. The resulting state in then passed to the command of the program.

As can be seen from this definition the output state of a program does not depend on its input state. This is, of course, only the consequence of our decision of not describing the input/output mechanism of Pascal. In a more realistic situation a state would contain an input file which then would have been accessed by input commands in "com".

6.2 TYPE EXPRESSIONS

Syntactically type expressions appear at the right-hand sides of type definitions and variable declarations. When a type expression is evaluated in a static environment we get a type.

$$TE : Type\text{-}exp \rightarrow Stat\text{-}env \rightarrow Type^E$$

The definition of TE is recursive with respect to the syntactic structure of type expressions. Cases in a recursive definition of a semantic function are called **semantic clauses**.

(TE.1) <u>Single-type-name expression</u>

    TE[t-name].s-env =
        t-name=boolean → (boolean),
        t-name=integer → (integer),
        t-nameεIde   →

$$(\text{t-name}\notin\text{dom.s-env} \quad \rightarrow \text{ERROR},$$
$$\text{s-env.t-name}=\text{EXPECTED} \rightarrow \text{ERROR},$$
$$\text{TRUE} \quad \rightarrow \text{s-env.t-name})$$

A standard name denotes the corresponding standard type. A type identifier denotes a type assigned to it in the current static environment.

(TE.2) <u>Record-type expression</u>

$$TE[\langle\text{v-dec}_1,\ldots,\text{v-dec}_n\rangle].\text{s-env} =$$
$$\textbf{let } \langle\langle\text{ide}_{i1},\ldots,\text{ide}_{im_i}\rangle,\text{t-exp}_i\rangle = \text{v-dec}_i \ ;$$
$$i = 1,\ldots,n \textbf{ in}$$
$$\textbf{let } \text{type}_i = TE[\text{t-exp}_i].\text{s-env} \ ; \ i=1,\ldots,n \textbf{ in}$$
$$(\exists i \leqslant n)(\text{type}_i=\text{ERROR}) \quad \rightarrow \text{ERROR},$$
$$(\exists i,j)(i\neq j \textbf{ and}$$
$$\text{field-ide.v-dec}_i \cap \text{field-ide.v-dec}_j\neq\{\}) \rightarrow \text{ERROR},$$
$$\text{TRUE} \quad \rightarrow \text{type}$$

where

$$\text{type} : \text{Record-type} = \text{Ide} \xrightarrow{m} \text{Var-descr}$$

and

$$\text{dom.type} = \text{field-ide.v-dec}_1|\ldots|\text{field-ide.v-dec}_n$$

and

$$(\forall i \leqslant n)(\forall j \leqslant m_i)$$
$$(\text{type.ide}_{ij} =$$
$$\text{t-exp}_i \varepsilon \text{Type-name} \rightarrow \text{mk-var-descr}(\text{type}_i),$$
$$\text{TRUE} \quad \rightarrow \text{mk-var-descr}(\langle\text{ide}_{ij},\text{type}_i\rangle)$$

The value of a record-type expression is a record type, hence a mapping from identifiers to variable descriptions. The domain of that mapping contains all and only field identifiers of all variable descriptions which appear in the expression. Moreover if

$$\langle\langle\text{ide}_{i1},\ldots,\text{ide}_{in}\rangle,\text{t-exp}_i\rangle$$

is a variables' declaration which appears in our expression, then the type assigned to each of ide_{ij} is a type denoted by $t\text{-}exp_i$ possibly named by ide_{ij}. The naming is applied whenever $t\text{-}exp_i$ is either a record-type or a pointer-type expression, i.e. *new type* in the terminology of STANDARD (cf. Sec.1).

(TE.3) <u>Pointer-type expression</u>

$$TE[mk\text{-}poit\text{-}t\text{-}exp(t\text{-}name)].s\text{-}env =$$
$$t\text{-}name\text{=}boolean \rightarrow mk\text{-}poiter\text{-}type((boolean)),$$
$$t\text{-}name\text{=}integer \rightarrow mk\text{-}poiter\text{-}type((integer)),$$
$$t\text{-}name\varepsilon Ide \quad\rightarrow mk\text{-}point\text{-}type((t\text{-}name))$$

Pointer-type expressions evaluate to fully defined types only for standard domain-types. For domain-types denoted by identifiers they return a pointer type with a parameter. As was explained in Sec.1 this model has been adopted for the description of circular types.

6.3 TYPE DEFINITIONS

Type definitions bind types — or the reserved symbol EXPECTED — to type identifiers in static environments. They may also generate and transmit error messages.

$$TD \; : \; Type\text{-}def \rightarrow Stat\text{-}env^E \rightarrow Stat\text{-}env^E$$

We assume that the denotations of type definitions are error preserving. For technical simplicity we omit in all subsequent definitions the case where ERROR is an argument of a denotation.

(TD.1) <u>Empty type definition</u>

$$TD[\langle\rangle].s\text{-}env = s\text{-}env$$

The denotation of an empty definition is the identity function on static environments.

(TD.2) <u>Single type-definition</u>

$$TD[<ide,t-exp>].s-env =$$

    let type = TE[t-exp].s-env **in**

    type=ERROR   → ERROR,

    ideϵdom.s-env   → ERROR,

    t-expϵType-name → s-env[type/ide],

    let $\{ide_1,..,ide_n\}$ =

            $\{ide' \mid$ ide'ϵdomain-types.type **and**

                ide'$\notin$types.s-env   **and**

                ide'$\neq$ide$\}$ **in**

    TRUE →

        s-env[$<$ide,type$>$/ide, EXPECTED/ide_1,...,EXPECTED/ide_n]

In the elaboration of a type definition we first evaluate the corresponding type expression t-exp. If this results in an error signal, then this signal is passed to the subsequent parts of the program. Otherwise we check whether the identifier which is being declared, has not been declared earlier. If that was the case, then another error signal is raised. Otherwise two cases may happen:

    1. t-exp may be either a standard-type name or an identifier in which case the (unlabeled) type denoted by t-exp is bound to ide in the static environment.

    2. t-exp may be either a record-type expression, or a pointer-type expression (*new type* in the sense of STANDARD) in which case the type denoted by t-exp labeled by ide is bound to ide and all domain-type identifiers in "type" which have not been defined yet are bound to EXPECTED.

(TD.3) <u>Compound type-definition</u>

$$TD[<t-def_1,t-def_2>] = TD[t-def_1] \cdot TD[t-def_2]$$

A sequence of type definitions is elaborated sequentially in the order determined by the syntax.

6.4 VARIABLE DECLARATIONS

Variable declarations bind types (marked by mk-var-descr) to identifiers in static environments, locations to (the same) identifiers in dynamic environments and pseudo-values of the corresponding types to (these) locations in stores.

$$VD : Var\text{-}dec \rightarrow State^E \rightarrow State^E$$

We assume that the denotations of variable declarations are error-reserving functions and we omit the case where ERROR is the argument of a denotation in our definition.

(VD.1) <u>Single variable-declaration</u>

$VD[\langle\langle ide_1,\ldots,ide_n\rangle,t\text{-}exp\rangle].\langle s\text{-}env,d\text{-}env,sto\rangle =$
    not repetition-free.$\langle ide_1,\ldots,ide_n\rangle \rightarrow$ ERROR,
    let type = TE[t-exp].s-env **in**
    type=ERROR $\rightarrow$ ERROR,
    $\{ide_1,\ldots,ide_n\} \cap$ dom.s-env$\neq\{\} \rightarrow$ ERROR,
    let type$'$ =
                  t-expεType-name $\rightarrow$ type,
                  TRUE $\rightarrow \langle ide_1,type\rangle$ **in**
    let s-env$'$ = s-env[mk-var-descr(type$'$)/ide_1,...
                          ...mk-var-descr(type$'$)/ide_n] **in**
    let $\langle loc_1,\ldots,loc_n\rangle$ = new.n.sto **in**
    let d-env$'$ = d-env[$loc_1/ide_1,\ldots,loc_n/ide_n$] **in**
    let sto$^\sim$ = sto[RESERVED/$loc_1,\ldots,$RESERVED/loc_n] **in**
    let sto$'$ = ($\langle$fill.loc_1.type.s-env$\cdot$
                 ...
           $\cdot$fill.loc_n.type.s-env).sto$^\sim$ **in**
  sto$'$=ERROR $\rightarrow$ ERROR.
  TRUE $\rightarrow \langle$s-env$'$,d-env$'$,sto$'\rangle$

In the elaboration of the declaration of variables we first check if the sequence of declared variables is repetition free. If this is not the case, then we signalize an error. Otherwise we evaluate type expression t-exp and if this does not lead to an error, then we check if all identifiers which are going to be declared have not been declared before. If it is not so, then error is signalized again. Otherwise we check if t-exp is a record—type—expression or a pointer—type—expression. In each of these cases we name (label) the type denoted by t-exp by ide_1. This is to fulfill the rule of STANDARD discussed in Sec.1. Next we modify the current static environment by binding appropriate variable descriptions to all declared identifiers. Then we modify the dynamic environment by choosing n fresh locations and assigning them to the declared identifiers. The last and the most complicated step consists in the modification of the store. This step is described in using an auxiliary function:

$$\text{fill} : \text{Loc} \rightarrow \text{Type} \rightarrow \text{Stat-env} \rightarrow \text{Store}^E \rightarrow \text{Store}^E$$

which given a location, a type, a static environment and a store modifies the store by filling the argument location with a pseudovalue which corresponds to the argument type seen in the context of the argument static environment. We assume that "fill" is error—preserving with respect to the last argument. It has the following recursive definition:

```
fill.loc.type.s-env.sto =
    type∈Standard-type → sto[RESERVED/loc],
    type∈Record-type   →
        let [v-descr₁/ide₁,...,v-descrₙ/ideₙ] = type in
        let typeᵢ = demark.v-descrᵢ ; i=1,...,n in
        let (loc₁,...,locₙ) = new.n.sto[RESERVED/loc] in
        let sto'=sto[[loc₁/ide₁,...,locₙ/ideₙ]/loc] in
        (fill.loc₁.type₁.s-env·
         ...
         •fill.locₙ.typeₙ.s-env).sto'
    type∈Pointer-type → sto[RESERVED/loc]
```

The location of a standard-type variable is filled with RESERVED. The location of a record-type variable is filled with an appropriate record, whose field locations are again filled by "fill" in a recursive manner. The location of a pointer-type variable is filled with RESERVED.

Observe that whereas the declaration of a record—type variable allocates a store space adequate for the corresponding record type, the declaration of a pointer—type variable allocates no space except of the single location associated to that variable. The generation of a full store space of a pointer variable can only be done by the command "new" (Sec.6.8).

(VD.2) Compound variable—declaration

$$VD[<v-dec_1,v-dec_2>] = VD[v-dec_1] \cdot VD[v-dec_2]$$

A sequence of variable declarations is elaborated sequentially in the order determined by the syntax.

6.5 THE CORRECTNESS PROPERTIES OF TYPE DEFINITIONS AND VARIABLE DECLARATIONS

As was mentioned in Sec.5 the denotations of type definitions and variable declarations are supposed to preserve the well—formedness of states. In this section we shall prove that fact thus showing the correctness of our definitions with respect to the predefined properties. In the considerations which follow we use the formalism introduced in Sec.10 of Part One.

Let us start from type definitions. By a simple inspection of (TD.2) one can check that the elaboration of a single type definition either raises an error signal or preserves the well—describedness of types (Sec.5.2). Since we have assumed that the denotations of type definitions are error—preserving the same remains true for compound type definitions. We can formulate therefore the following correctness statements:

   totpre well—described—types: (6.1)
      TD[t—def]
   totpost if no—error **then** well—described—types **fi**

where "no—error" is the following generic function defined for every domain Dom:

```
no-error : Dom^E → Boolerr
no-error.dom = dom≠ERROR → tt, ff
```

Now let us proceed to the properties of variable declarations. As one may easilly check, the function "fill" has been defined in such a way that it fulfills the reqirements expressed by the predicate well-filled (Sec.5.2). In fact, that predicate may be regarded as a logical specification of "fill". Formally one may prove that for every loc, type, s-env and sto, the following is true:

$$
\begin{array}{ll}
\textbf{if} & \hspace{5cm} (6.2)\\
\quad \text{well-filled-types.s-env} \\
\textbf{then} \\
\quad \textbf{let}\ sto' = \text{fill.loc.type.s-env.sto}\ \textbf{in} \\
\quad \textbf{if} \\
\quad\quad \text{domain-types.type}\ \varepsilon\ \text{types.s-env} \\
\quad \textbf{then} \\
\quad\quad \text{well-filled.loc.type.s-env.sto'} \\
\quad \textbf{else} \\
\quad\quad sto' = \text{ERROR} \\
\quad \textbf{fi} \\
\textbf{fi}
\end{array}
$$

The proof of that fact is very simple and proceeds by comparing all successive cases in the definition of "fill" with the corresponding cases in the definition of "well-filled". It is understood that

if p **then** q **else** r **fi**

is an abbreviation of

if p **then** q **fi and if not** p **then** r **fi**

On the strength of (6.2) we can further prove the following:

$$
\begin{array}{ll}
\textbf{totpre}\ \text{well-formed-state} & \hspace{4cm} (6.3)\\
\quad VD[\langle\langle ide_1,\ldots,ide_n\rangle,t\text{-exp}\rangle] \\
\textbf{totpost if}\ \text{no-error}\ \textbf{then}\ \text{well-formed-state}\ \textbf{fi}
\end{array}
$$

Since the denotations of variable declarations are error-preserving functions, the above correctness statement can easily be generalized to arbitrary, i.e. possibly compound, variable declarations:

> **totpre** well-formed-state   (6.4)
>   VD[v-dec]
> **totpost** if no-error **then** well-formed-state **fi**

Note. The function "fill" has been defined in such a way that it returns an error signal whenever "type" is a pointer-type with an undefined domain-type. This case has been included for the completeness of our definition, but it will never appear in program execution since on the strength of (6.1) and (6.4) variable declarations are always elaborated in states with well-described types.

End of note

So far we have been dealing with the preserveness of the well-formedness of states by type definitions and variable declarations. Now we shall prove that the block of type definitions and variable declarations which appears at the beginning of every program always creates either a well-formed state or an error message. In order to provide a lucid formulation of the corresponding correctness statement we first extend error-preserving functions and predicates on static environments to error-preserving functions and predicates on states. This will allow us to formally combine correctness statements about type definitions with these for variable declarations. For any function and predicate:

> f : Stat-env^E $\not\rightarrow$ Stat-env^E
> p : Stat-env^E $\rightarrow$ Boolerr

we define

> $f^\sim$: State^E $\rightarrow$ State^E
> $p^\sim$: State^E $\rightarrow$ Boolerr

such that

> $f^\sim$.⟨s-env,d-env,sto⟩ =
> f.s-env=ERROR $\rightarrow$ ERROR
>   TRUE $\rightarrow$ ⟨f.s-env,d-env,sto⟩

```
p~.<s-env,d-env,sto> = p.s-env
```

Furthermore, for every predicate p on states we define the following error-preserving function:

$$\text{test.p : State}^E \to \text{State}^E$$

```
test.p.sta = p.sta=ff → ERROR, sta
```

Finally, we define an error-preserving function and a predicate on states:

```
clear : State → State
no-variables : State → Boolerr
```

such that

```
clear.sta = <[],[],[]>

no-variables.<s-env,d-env,sto> =
    variables.s-env={} and d-env=[] and sto=[] → tt, ff
```

In this new notation we can rewrite the semantic clause for programs of Sec.6.1 in the following form:

```
P[<t-def,v-dec,com>] =
      clear
   • TD[t-def]~
   • test.(no-types-expected~)
   • VD[v-dec]
   • C[com]
```

Now we can formulate four simple correctness statements:

totpre tt
      clear
totpost no-variables **and** well-described-types~

This statement is obvious since every empty state trivially satisfies this postcondition.

totpre no-variables **and** well-described-types~
    TD[t-def]~
totpost no-variables **and if** no-error **then**
    well-described-types~ **fi**

This follows immediately from (6.1).

totpre no-variables **and if** no-error **then**
    well-described-types~ **fi**
test.(no-types-expected~)
totpost no-variables **and if** no-error **then**
    well-formed-state **fi**

This is true because if there are no variables declared in a state
then "well-described-types" and "no-types-expected" is all what we
require for the fell-formedness of a state.

totpre if no-error **then** well-formed-state **fi**
    VD[v-dec]
totpost if no-error **then** well-formed-state **fi**

This follows from (6.4) and the preservation of error by variable
declarations.

From these four intermediate correctness statements we can infer a
final one in using proof rules (TC-1) and (TC-5) of Sec.10 in Part
One:

totpre tt   (6.5)
        clear
    • TD[t-def]~
    • test.(no-types-expected~)
    • VD[v-dec]
totpost if no-error **then** well-formed-state **fi**

This statement formalizes our former claim that the block of type
definitions and variable declarations which appears at the beginning
of every program always creates either a well-formed state or an
error message.

6.6 EXPRESSIONS

There are two types of expressions in our language: left expressions and right-expressions. The former appear on the left-hand sides of assignments and in commands **new** and **dispose**. In full Pascal they appear also as actual reference-parameters in procedure calls. The latter appear on the righ-hand sides of assignments and in full Pascal also as actual value-parameters in procedure calls. When we evaluate a left expression we receive a location as a value. The value of a right expression may be any element of the algebra of data types.

As is easy to see from the syntax of the language, expressions are never evaluated prior to the elaboration of type definitions and variable declarations. It will be also seen later that expression evaluation does not lead to any side-effects, i.e. does not change states, and that the execution of commands never destroys the well-formedness of states. From all these facts we can conclude on the ground of (6.5) that expressions are always evaluated in well-formed states. This observation allows us for the replacement of some run-time checks in the semantic clauses of expressions by less expensive static checks. This will be seen in Sec.6.6.3 and Sec.6.7.

In order to describe the mentioned mechanism of static checks we define an auxiliary semantic function which evaluates expressions to types.

6.6.1 The type of an expression

In this section we define a function:

$$TY : Exp \rightarrow Stat\text{-}env \rightarrow Type^E$$

which given an expression and a static environment returns the type of the expected (dynamic) value of that expression.

(TY.1) <u>Single-identifier expression</u>

```
TY[ide].s-env =
    ide∉dom.s-env          → ERROR,
    s-env.ide∉Var-descr → ERROR,
    TRUE                   → demark.(s-env.ide)
```

(TY.2) <u>Field designator</u>

```
TY[<l-exp,ide>].s-env =
    let type = TY[l-exp].s-env in
    type=ERROR              → ERROR,
    let type' = remove-name.type in
    type'∉Record-type → ERROR,
    ide∉dom.type'          → ERROR,
    TRUE                   → demark.(type'.ide)
```

(TY.3) <u>Dereferenced expression</u>

```
TY[mk-deref(l-exp)].s-env =
    let type = TY[l-exp].s-env in
    type = ERROR            → ERROR,
    let type' = remove-name.type in
    type'∉Pointer-type → ERROR
    TRUE                   → demark.type'
```

(TY.4) <u>Constant arithmetic expression</u>

```
TY[one].s-env = (integer)
```

(TY.5) <u>Plus expression</u>

```
TY[mk-plus-exp(<a-exp₁,a-exp₂>)].s-env =
    let type₁ = TY[a-exp₁].s-env in
    let type₂ = TY[a-exp₂].e-env in
    type₁=type₂=(integer) → (integer)
    TRUE                          → ERROR
```

(TY.6) <u>A constant Boolean expression</u>

    TY[true].s-env = (boolean)

(TY.7) <u>And expression</u>

    analogous to (TY.5)

6.6.2 Left expressions

In a given state a left expression denotes a location which indicates where an appropriate state transformation is going to take place. Formally, the semantics of left expressions is the following function:

    L : Left-expression $\rightarrow$ State $\rightarrow$ Loc^E

(L.1) <u>Single-identifier l-expression</u>

    L[ide].<s-env,d-env,sto> =
       ide∉dom.d-env $\rightarrow$ ERROR,
       TRUE $\rightarrow$ d-env.ide

(L.2) <u>Field designator</u>

    L[<l-exp,ide>].<s-env,d-env,sto> =
       let loc = L[l-exp].<s-env,d-env,sto> **in**
       loc=ERROR $\rightarrow$ ERROR,
       let val = sto.loc **in**
       val∉Rec $\rightarrow$ ERROR,
       ide∉dom.val $\rightarrow$ ERROR,
       TRUE $\rightarrow$ val.ide

(L.3) <u>Dereferenced expression</u>

    L[mk-deref(l-exp)].<s-env,d-env,sto> =
       let loc = L[l-exp].<s-env,d-env,sto> **in**
       loc=ERROR $\rightarrow$ ERROR,

```
let p-val = sto.loc in
p-val∉Loc → ERROR,
TRUE       → p-val
```

6.6.3 Right expressions

In a given state a right expression denotes an element of the algebra of data types. The semantics of right expressions is therefore defined as the following function:

$$R : Right\text{-}exp \to State \to Value^E$$

As we mentioned already at the beginning of Sec.6.6, expressions are always evaluated in well-formed states. This allows us to replace some run-time checks performed with the access to the whole state, by less expensive compile-time checks performed with the access to the static environment only. Formally, we assume that R[exp] always returns ERROR for non-well-formed states and in the definition of R we refer to TY whenever we have to check the type of a subexpression.

(R.1) <u>A left expression as a right expression</u>

```
R[l-exp].<s-env,d-env,sto> =
    let loc = L[l-exp].<s-env,d-env,sto> in
    loc=ERROR        → ERROR,
    sto.loc∉Value → ERROR
    TRUE             → sto.loc
```

(R.2) <u>Constant arithmetic r-expression</u>

```
R[one].sta = 1
```

(R.3) <u>Plus expression</u>

```
R[mk-plus-exp(<a-exp₁,a-exp₂>).<s-env,d-env,sto> =
    let type₁ = TY[a-exp₁].s-env in
    let type₂ = TY[a-exp₂].s-env in
    type₁≠(integer) or type₂≠(integer) → ERROR,
```

```
let i₁ = R[a-exp₁].<s-env,d-env,sto> in
let i₂ = R[a-exp₂].<s-env,d-env,sto> in
i₁=ERROR or i₂=ERROR                    → ERROR,
TRUE                                    → plus.<i₁,i₂>
```

Observe that in this definition we only check the types of $a\text{-}exp_i$ and on that ground (since our state is well formed) we conclude that i_1 and i_2 are integers and we apply the function "plus" to them.

(R.4) <u>Constant Boolean expressions</u>

    R[true].sta = (true)

(R.5) <u>And expression</u>

```
R[mk-and-exp(<b-exp₁,b-exp₂>).<s-env,d-env,sto> =
    let type₁ = TY[b-exp₁].s-env in
    let type₂ = TY[b-exp₂].s-env in
    type₁≠(boolean) or type₂≠(boolean) → ERROR,
    let b₁ = R[a-exp₁].<s-env,d-env,sto> in
    let b₂ = R[a-exp₂].<s-env,d-env,sto> in
    b₁=ERROR or b₂=ERROR                    → ERROR,
    TRUE                                    → and.<b₁,b₂>
```

The same remark as in (R.3) applies here.

6.7 THE TYPE-CORRECTNESS OF EXPRESSIONS

Types in programming languages serve three main purposes: (1) they help in memory allocation, (2) they allow for static detection of some errors, and finally (3) they introduce redundancy into the language thus helping the programmer to avoid some errors. Of course, in order to really serve these purposes, the mechanism of types must be sufficiently adequate. In particular, the following properties must be satisfied:

1) The program prefix of type definitions and variable declarations must always produce well-formed states.

2) Commands must never destroy the well-formedness of states.

3) The values (in states) of expressions must always coincide with the types of these expressions.

The satisfaction of 1) has been shown in Sec.6.5. The satisfaction of 2) will be discussed in Sec.6.9. Here we deal with property 3). In order to formulate it we introduce an auxiliary function:

    carrier-of : Type → Value-set

    carrier-of.type =
        type=(boolean) → Bool,
        type=(integer) → Int,
        typeεRec-type →
            let [v-descr$_1$/ide$_1$,...,v-descr$_n$/ide$_n$] = type in
            {[loc$_1$/ide$_1$,...,loc$_n$/ide$_n$] | loc$_i\varepsilon$Loc}
        typeεPointer-type → Loc

Now we can formulate property 3):

    ($\forall$<s-env,d-env,sto>)   (6.6)
    let type = TY[exp].s-env in
    let val = R[exp].<s-env,d-env,sto> in
    if well-formed-state.<s-env,d-env,sto>
        then
            if type$\neq$ERROR and val$\neq$ERROR
                then val ε carrier-of.type
            fi
    fi

This formula is seemingly very weak since the function "carrier-of" is gluing very many non-standard types together (cf. Sec.1 and Sec.4.3). In fact, however, in the context of the well-formedness of a state it says everything what one can say about Pascal values. Consider the following example of a variable declaration:

    var
        p:record
            x:integer;
            y:record v:integer; b:boolean end
        end

The satisfaction of (6.6) for p regarded as an expression means that for every state sta

$$R[p].sta = [loc_1/x,...,loc_n/y]$$

for some loc_1 and loc_2. Now, if sta is well-formed, then we can conclude that loc_1 is filled either with an integer or with RESERVED and loc_2 is filled with an appropriate well-filled record.

6.8 COMMANDS

Commands transform states by modifying their store component. Of course, they may also raise and transmit error messages. Since commands contain a loop construction, the denotation of a command is in general a partial function:

$$C : Com \rightarrow State^E \not\rightarrow State^E$$

Of course, we assume as usual that the denotations of commands are error preserving and we omit the case where ERROR is an argument in our definitions.

(C.1.1) <u>Assignment command</u> (excluding a nil-to-pointer assignment)

```
C[mk-assign(<l-exp,r-exp>].<s-env,d-env,sto> =
    let type₁ = TY[l-exp].s-env in
    let type₂ = TY[l-exp].s-env in
    type₁=ERROR or type₂=ERROR → ERROR,
    type₁≠type₂              → ERROR,
    let loc = L[l-exp].<s-env,d-env,sto> in
    let val   R[r-exp].<s-env,d-env,sto> in
    loc=ERROR or val=ERROR   → ERROR,
    let sto' = assign.loc.val.sto in
    sto'=ERROR               → ERROR,
    TRUE                     → (s-env,d-env,sto')
```

where "assign" is the following error-preserving recursively defined function:

$$\text{assign} : \text{Loc} \rightarrow \text{Pseudo-value} \rightarrow \text{Store}^E \rightarrow \text{Store}^E$$

```
assign.loc.p-val.sto =
    p-val=RESERVED  → ERROR,
    p-val=NIL       → ERROR,
    p-valεBool|Int|Loc → sto[p-val/loc]
    let [loc₁/ide₁,...,locₙ/ideₙ] = p-val in
    sto.loc∉Rec    → ERROR,
    let [loc′₁/ide₁,...,loc′ₘ/ideₘ] = sto.loc in
    n≠m                 → ERROR,
    TRUE                → (assign.loc′₁.(sto.loc₁)•
                          ...
                         •assign.loc′ₙ.(sto.locₙ)).sto
```

In REPORT the semantics of assignment is described in the following
way:

*"The assignment statement serves to replace the current value of
a variable by a new value specified as an expression."*

As we see from (C.1.1) the situation is much more complicated. This
is partly due to type-compatibility requirements, but the bulk of the
work must be done when one assigns a record to a record variable.
This is the consequence of our location-oriented model of records
which in turn has been forced by Pascal mechanism of passing
variables as parameters (cf. the corresponding remarks of Sec.1). Of
course, in full Pascal where records may have variants, the situation
is even worse (cf. [Andrews, Henhapl 82]).

In defining the abstract syntax of assignments in Sec.3 we have
deliberately separated the case where "nil" is assigned to a pointer
variable. This decision is purely technical. It only allows us to
exclude "nil" from the set of expressions thus avoiding a rather
inelegant situation where TY is used to calculate the type of "nil".

(C.1.2) <u>A nil-to-pointer assignment</u>

```
C[mk-assign(<l-exp,nil>).<s-env,d-env,sto> =
    let type = TY[l-exp].s-env in
    type∉Pointer-type → ERROR,
    let loc = L[l-exp].<s-env,d-env,sto> in
```

```
        loc=ERROR              → ERROR,
        TRUE                   → sto[NIL/loc]
```

This command only assigns NIL to the location denoted by the pointer-expression l-exp. In other words, it initializes the pointer denoted by l-exp by giving it the value NIL.

(C.2) A new-pointer command

```
    C[mk-new(l-exp)].<s-env,d-env,sto> =
        let type = TY[l-exp].s-env in
        type≠Pointer-type → ERROR,
        let type^d = demark.type in
        let loc = L[l-exp].<s-env,d-env,sto> in
        loc=ERROR              → ERROR,
        let loc' = new.1.sto in
        let sto' = fill.loc'.type^d.s-env.(sto[loc'/loc]) in
        TRUE                   → <s-env,d-env,sto'>
```

This command modifies the store by assigning a new location loc' to the location loc of the pointer and then by filling this new location with an uninitialized memory structure corresponding to the domain type of the pointer. The filling procedure is the same as in variable declarations and therefore we are using here the function "fill" defined in Sec.6.4. Notice, however, that in elaborating a pointer declaration (VD.1 in Sec.6.4) we do not enter the "fill" procedure, but only associate RESERVE to the location of the pointer.

(C.3) Disposing a pointer

```
    C[mk-dispose(l-exp)].<s-env,d-env,sto> =
        let type = TY[l-exp].s-env in
        type≠Pointer-type → ERROR,
        let loc = L[l-exp].<s-env,d-env,sto> in
        loc=ERROR              → ERROR,
        TRUE                   → <s-env,d-env,sto[RESERVED/loc]>
```

This command replaces the value denoted by the pointer l-exp by the undefinedness symbol RESERVED. In that way the region of the memory (i.e. the dynamic structure) so far accessible via l-exp becomes inaccessible via l-exp. This fulfills the STANDARD requirement that the execution of dispose command:

"*shall remove the identifying value denoted by the expression* l-exp *from the pointer type of* l-exp."

On the other hand our definition hardly meets the expectations which the reader of the manual part of [Wilson, Addyman 82] may associate to dispose command after having read the explanation given in that manual:

"*The procedure* **dispose** *is an inverse of* **new**. (...) *Its action in to remove the pointer value from its type, thereby making the unwanted variable inaccessible. This allows the storage space allocated to the variable to be recovered for the future use.*"

It is quite clear that our definition does not meet the above explanation since it only guarantees that the dispose variable has no access to its former storage space while it does not affect other pointer variables which might have head access to the same storage space or to some parts of it. If there are such variables, then the storage space in question cannot be recovered for future use! Consider the following example:

```
type
    link = ↑list;
    list = record x:integer; l:link end
var
    p,q,r:link;
begin
    new(p);
    new(q);
    p↑.l := q;
    q := p;
    r := p↑.l;
    dispose(p);
    ...
```

According to our definition (and to the literal meaning of STANDARD's definition of "dispose") the execution of dispose(p) only cuts the access trough p to the created list, whereas this list can still be accessed trough q and part of this list through r. In this situation the storage space of the list cannot be recovered for future use.

(C.4) <u>If command</u>

$$C[mk-if(<b-exp,com_1,com_2>)].sta =$$
    let val = R[b-exp].sta **in**
    val$\notin$Bool $\rightarrow$ ERROR,
    val=(true) $\rightarrow$ $C[com_1]$.sta,
    val=(false) $\rightarrow$ $C[com_2]$.sta

(C.5) <u>While command</u>

$$C[mk-while(<b-exp,com>)].sta =$$
    let val = R[b-exp].sta **in**
    val$\notin$Bool $\rightarrow$ ERROR,
    val=(true) $\rightarrow$ $(C[com_1] \bullet C[mk-while(<b-exp,com>)]).sta,$
    val=(false) $\rightarrow$ sta

(C.6) <u>Compound command</u>

$$C[<com_1,com_2>] = C[com_1] \bullet C[com_2]$$

We do not comment the last three clauses since they are quite
routine.

6.9 THE CORRECTNESS PROPERTIES OF COMMANDS

The only correctness statement which we formulate about commands is
that they do not destroy the well-formedness of states. Formally:

    parpre well-formed-state   (6.7)
      C[com]
    parpost if no-error **then** well-formed-state **fi**

Notice that in contrast to the correctness statements for definitions
and declarations this time we have only a partial-correctness
property. This is, of course, the consequence of the fact that

command denotations are in general partial functions. In other words, the well-formedness of an input state does not guarantee the termination of a command execution.

The sketch of the proof of (6.7) is following: Since commands change only stores, all we have to prove is the preservation of well-allocadedness of variables. For assignments (C.1.1) and (C.1.2), new-pointer generation (C.2) and dispose command (C.3) this leads to a technically tedious, but logically simple case checking. For other cases we have an obvious structural induction.

THE DERIVATION OF PROGRAM-CORRECTNESS PROOF RULES

This section is devoted to the derivation of program-correctness proof rules for a programming language which has a denotational definition. We derive a few example rules for our subset of Pascal and we discuss some associated general problems.

The derivation of a program-correctness proof system must be preceded by the development of an appropriate language of conditions. Semantically conditions should denote predicates on states. Since the construction of a language of conditions is a rather routine task (cf. [de Bakker 80]) we shall not treat it in details. We only assume that our conditions have a few simple properties. Let

   cond : Cond = ...

be the syntactic domain of conditions, and let

   CD : Cond → State^E → Boolerr

be the corresponding function of semantics. We assume that CD is defined over McCarthy's predicate calculus (Sec.9 of Part One) and that CD[cond].ERROR = ee. About Cond we assume that it contains all Boolean expressions and that it is closed (although it does not need to be the least closed) under propositional connectives and quantifiers. We assume also that this class is closed under the operation of the substitution of right expressions for left expressions. In the sequel we shall use a function:

   sub : Cond x Left-exp x Right-exp → Cond

where sub.(cond,l-exp,r-exp), denoted for short by cond[r-exp/l-exp], is the result of the substitution of r-exp for each free occurrence of l-exp in cond. If cond contains no free occurrence of l-exp, then cond[r-exp/l-exp] = cond. The substitution must be defined in such a

way that for every condition cond, left expression l-exp, right
expression r-exp and a state sta the following implication is true:

(7.1)

```
if C[l-exp := r-exp].sta ≠ ERROR
    then
        let loc = L[l-exp].sta in
        let val = R[r-exp].sta in
        let <s-env,d-env,sto> = sta in
        CD[cond[r-exp/l-exp]].sta =
        = CD[cond].<s-env,d-env,sto[val/loc]>
fi
```

We need this property for the further derivation of a proof rule for
the command of assignment.

After having extended our programming language by conditions we may
proceed to the development of proof rules. We shall concentrate on
total-correctness proof rules (cf.Sec.10 of Part One) which are
appropriate for typical Pascal applications where a program does a
certain job and then stops. Let us start from a rule for assignment.

For every assignment mk-assign(<l-exp,r-exp>), every precondition
$cond_{pr}$ and every postcondition $cond_{po}$:

```
    totpre CD[cond_pr] and well-formed-state                    (7.2)
        C[mk-assign(l-exp,r-exp)]
    totpost CD[cond_po] and well-formed-state
    ========================================================
    (∀sta∈State)
    let <s-env,d-env,sto> = sta in
    if well-formed-state.sta and CD[cond_pr].sta
        then
            TY[l-exp].s-env = TY[r-exp].s-env ≠ ERROR and
            L[l-exp].sta ≠ ERROR                          and
            R[r-exp].sta ≠ ERROR                          and
            CD[cond_po[r-exp/l-exp]].sta
    fi
```

This rule may be read as follows:

the satisfaction of the precondition $cond_{pr}$ and the well-formedness of a state implies the (clean) termination of the assignment, the well-formedness of the output state and the satisfaction of the postcondition $cond_{po}$ in that state.

IF AND ONLY IF

in every well-formed state the satisfaction of the precondition $cond_{pr}$ implies the following:
1. the types of l-exp and r-exp are correct and equal,
2. the left value of l-exp and the right value of r-exp are defined,
3. the modified postcondition $cond_{po}[r-exp/l-exp]$ is satisfied,

The proof of that rule follows from the semantic clause of assignment command (C.1), the preservation of the well-formedness of states by commands (6.7) and the assumed property of substitution (7.1).

Now we shall formulate a rule for a new-pointer-generation command mk-new(l-exp). For simplicity we shall restrict ourselves to the case where l-exp is an identifier. The generalization of this case to arbitrary left expressions is left to the reader.

First we make another assumption about the set of conditions. We assume that for any ideϵIde, this set contains a condition which we denote by new-pointer.ide and which has the following semantics:

```
CD[new-pointer.ide].<s-env,d-env,sto> =
    d-env.ideεLoc          and
    sto.(d-env.ide)εLoc and
    s-env.ideεVar-descr and
    let type = demark.(s-env.ide) in
    let type₁ = remove-name.type in
    type₁εPointer-type   and
    let d-name = demark.type₁ in
    let type₂ =
            d-nameεStandard-type → d-name
            TRUE                 → TE[d-name].s-env
    well-filled.(sto.(d-env.ide)).type₂.s-env.sto
```

The satisfaction of new-pointer.ide means that ide is a variable identifier of pointer type and that this variable has been assigned a memory space adequate for the domain type of that pointer type. Now the proof rule for our command is the following. For any mk-new(ide), $cond_{pr}$ and $cond_{po}$:

> **totpre** CD[$cond_{pr}$] **and** well-formed-state   (7.3)
>   C[mk-new(ide)]
> **totpost** CD[($\exists$ide)$cond_{pr}$] **and**
>   CD[new-pointer.ide] **and**
>   well-formed-state

===

> ($\forall$staεState)
>   **let** <s-env,d-env,sto> = sta **in**
>   **if** well-formed-state **and** CD[$cond_{pr}$].sta
>   **then**
>   TY[ide].s-envεPointer-type
>   **fi**

This rule can be read as follows:

> *the satisfaction of the precondition and the well-formedness of a state imply the (clean) termination of mk-new(ide) command, the well-formedness of a terminal state, the satisfaction of the new-pointer property for ide and the satisfaction of the precondition existentially quantified over ide*

IF AND ONLY IF

> *the precondition and the well-formedness of the current state imply that ide denotes a pointer,*

The existential quantification of ide in the postcondition reflects the fact that after the execution of mk-new(ide), ide denotes a noninitialized pointer variable.

The development of proof rules for the remaining commands of our subset of Pascal is left to the reader. The rules for assigning NIL to a pointer and for disposing a pointer seem quite easy. The rules for mk-if(b-exp,com$_1$,com$_2$>) and <com$_1$,com$_2$> follow immediately from the general rules (TC-1) and (TC-3) in Sec.10 of

Part One. The rule for mk-while(<b-exp,com>) is slightly more complicated. Its formulation requires the introduction of a language of so called **termination expressions** and an appropriate extension of our language of conditions. For details the reader may wish to consult [Blikle 81a].

REFERENCES

ANDREWS, D., HENHAPL, W.,

[82] **Pascal**, in: Bjørner, D., Jones C., Formal Specification
and Software Development, Prentice Hall Int. 1982

de BAKKER, J.

[80] **Mathematical Theory of Program Correctness**, Prentice Hall
Int. 1980

BARENDREGT, H.P.

[84] **The Lambda Calculus, its Syntax and Semantics**, in:
Studies in Logic and the Foundations of Mathematics, Vol.103,
North Holland (1984), revised edition.

BARRINGER, H., CHENG, J.H., JONES C.B.

[84] **A logic covering undefinedness in program proofs**, Acta
Informatica 21 (1984), 251–269

BJØRNER, D., JONES, C.B.

[78] **The Vienna Development Method: The Meta Language**, LNCS
Vol.61, Springer Verlag 1978
[82] **Formal Specification and Software Development**, Prentice
Hall Int. 1982

BJØRNER, D. OEST, O.N. (eds.)

[80] **Towards a Formal Description of Ada**, LNCS 98, Springer
Verlag 1980

BJØRNER, D., PREHN, S.

[83] **Software engineering aspects of VDM; the Vienna Development
Method**, in: Theory and Practice of Software Technology
(D.Ferrari, M.Bolognani, J.Goguen, eds.) North–Holland 1983

BLIKLE A.

[71] **Iterative systems; an algebraic approach**, Bull. Acad.
Polon. Sci., Sér. Sci. Math. Astronom. et Phys. 20 (1971),
51–55
[72] **Complex iterative systems**, ibid. 21 (1972), 57–61
[72a] **Equational languages**, Information and Control, 21 (1972),
134–147
[74] **Proving programs by delta relations**, in: Formalization of
Programming Languages and Writing of Compilers (Proc. Symp.
Frankfurt/Oder 1974), Elektronische Informationsverarbeitung
und Kybernetik 11 (1975), 267–274
[77] **An analysis of programs by algebraic means**, in:
Mathematical Foundations of Computer Science (Proc. S.Banach

Semester, Winter 1974), Banach Center Publications Vol.2,
Polish Scientific Publishers 1977

[77a] **An analytic approach to the verification of iterative
programs**, in: Information Processing (Proc. IFIP Congress
1977, B.Gilchrist ed.), North Holland 1977, 285–290

[77b] **A comparative review of some program–verification
methods**, MFCS 1977 (Proc. 6th Symp., Tatranska Lomnica 1977),
LNCS Vol.53, Springer Verlag 1977, 17–33

[78] **Specified programming**, in: Mathematical Studies of
Information Processing (Proc. Conf. Kyoto 1978, eds. K.E.Blum,
M.Paul, S.Takasu), LNCS Vol.75, Springer Verlag 1979

[81] **On the development of correct specified programs**, IEEE
Trans. on Soft. Eng. SE–7 (1981), 519–527

[81a] **The clean termination of iterative programs**, Acta
Informatica 16 (1981), 199–217

[81b] **Notes on the mathematical semantics of programming
languages**, Technical Report LiTH–MAT–R–81–19, Linkoeping 1981

[82] **Desophisticating denotational semantics**, a manuscript
1982

[83] **A metalanguage for naive denotational semantics**, Progetto
Finalizzato Informatica, CNR Progetto P, Cnet 104, Pisa 1983

[87] **Denotational engineering, or from denotations to syntax**,
in: VDM – A Formal Method at Work, (Proc.VDM–Europe Symposium
1987, Brussels, March 1987, D.Bjørner, C.B.Jones, M.Mac an
Airchinnigh, E.J.Neuhold eds.), LNCS 252, Springer 1987

BLIKLE, A., MAZURKIEWICZ, A.

[72] **An algebraic approach to the theory of programs
algorithms, languages and recursiveness**, MFCS 1972 (Proc.
Conf., Warszawa–Jablonna 1972), Warsaw 1972

BLIKLE, A., TARLECKI, A.

[83] **Naive denotational semantics**, in: Information Processing
83 (Proc. IFIP Congress 1983, R.E.A.Manson ed.), North Holland
1983

COHN, P.M.

[81] **Universal Algebra**, D.Reidel Publishing Company 1981

EHRIG, H., MAHR B.,

[85] **Fundamentals of Algebraic Specification 1**, Springer
Verlag 1985

CURRY, H.B., FEYS, R.

[58] **Combinatory Logic**, Vol.1, North Holland 1958

FLOYD, R.W.

[67] **Assigning meanings to programs**, in: Mathematical Aspects
of Computer Science, (Proc. Symp. Applied Math., J.T.Schwartz
ed), American Mathematical Society 1967

FREUDENTAL, H.

[73] **Mathematics as an Education Task**, Dorendrecht 1973

GOGUEN, J.A.

[77] **Abstract errors for abstract data types**, in: Formal
      Description of Programming Concepts (Proc. IFIP Working
      Conference, 1977, E.Neuhold ed.), North Holland 1978

GOGUEN, J.A., THATCHER. J.W., WAGNER, E.G., WRIGHT J.B.

[77] **Initial algebra semantics and continuous algebras**, IBM
      Research Report RC-5701, Nov.1975, since then published in
      JACM, 24 (1977), 68-95

GORDON, M.J.C.

[79] **The Denotational Description of Programming Languages**,
      Springer Verlag 1979

HARRISON, M.A.

[78] **Introduction to Formal Language Theory**, Addison-Wesley
      Publishing Company 1978

HITCHCOCK, P., PARK, D.

[72] **Induction rules and termination proofs**, in: Automata,
      Languages and Programming, (Proc. IRIA Symp. 1972, M.Nivat
      ed.), North Holland 1973, 225-252

HOARE, C.A.R.

[69] **An axiomatic basis for computer programming**,
      Communications of ACM 12 (1969), 576-583

HOOGEWIJS, A.

[79] **On a formalization of the non-definedness notion**,
      Zeitschrift f. Math. Logik u. Grundlagen d. Math. Vol.25
      (1979), 213-221
[83] **A partial predicate calculus in a two-valued logic**, ibid.
      Vol.29 (1983), 239-243
[87] **Partial-predicate logic in computer science**, Acta
      Informatica, Vol.24, (1987), 381-394

JENSEN, K., WIRTH, N.,

[75] **PASCAL; User Manual**, Second Edition, Springer Verlag 1975

JONES, C.B.

[78] **Denotational semantics of goto: an exit formulation and
      its relation to continuations**, in: The Vienna Development
      Method, The Metalanguage (D.Bjørner, C.B.Jones eds.), LNCS
      Springer Verlag 1978

KLEENE, S.C.

[38] **On notation for ordinal numbers**, Journal of Symb. Logic,
      Vol.3 (1938), 150-155
[52] **Introduction to Metamathematics**, North Holland 1952;
      since then republished in 1957, 59, 62, 64, 67, 71

LUKASIEWICZ, J.

[20] **O logice trójwartosciowej** (On three-valued logic), Ruch
Filozoficzny, Vol.5, Lwow 1920, 169-171

MANNA, A., PNUELI, A.

[74] **Axiomatic approach to total correctness of programs**, Acta
Informatica (1974)

MARCISZEWSKI, W.

[87] **Systems of computer-aided reasoning for mathematical and
natural language**, in: Initiative in Logic (J.Srzednicki,
ed.), Martinus Nijhof, Dordrecht 1987

MAZURKIEWICZ, A.

[72] **Iteratively computable relations**, Bull. Acad. Polon.
Sci., Sér. Sci. Math. Astronom. et Phys. Vol.20 (1972),
793-797
[73] **Proving properties of processes**, an invited lecture at
MFCS 1973, since then published in Algorytmy 11 (1974), 5-22

McCARTHY, J.

[61] **A basis for a mathematical theory of computation.** Western
Joint Computer Conference, May 1961, since then published in
Computer Programming and Formal Systems (P.Braffort,
D.Hirshberg eds.), North Holland 1967, 33-70

MOSSES, P.D.,

[74] **The mathematical semantics of Algol 60**, Technical
Monograph PRG-12, Oxford University 1974

RASIOWA, H.

[74] **An Algebraic Approach to Non-Classical Logic**,
North-Holland 1974

SCOTT, D.

[71] **Continuous lattices**, in: Toposets, Algebraic Geometry and
Logic; Proc. 1971 Dalhousie Conference (F.W.Lawvere ed.), LNM
Springer Verlag 274 (1972), 97-136
[76] **Data types as lattices**, SIAM Journal on Computing, Vol.5
(1976), 522-587

STOY, J.E.

[77] **Denotational Semantics: The Scott-Strachey Approach to
Programming Language Theory**, The MIT Press, Cambridge Mass.
1977

STRACHEY, C., WADSWORTH, C.P.

[74] **Continuations, a mathematical semantics for handling full
jumps**, Technical Monograph PRG-11, Oxford 1974

TENNENT, R.D.

[76] **The denotational semantics of programming languages,**
Communication of ACM, Vol.19 (1976), 437–453

TURING, A.

[49] **On checking a large routine,** Report of a Conference on
High Speed Calculating Machines, University Mathematical
Laboratory, Cambridge 1949, 67–69

WILSON, I.R., ADDYMAN, A.M.

[82] **A Practical Introduction to Pascal with BS 6192,**
Macmillan Computer Science Series, Second Edition, 1982

WORONOWICZ, E.

[86] **Supporting the process of correct–programs construction in
an experimental computer environment,** (in Polish), a Ph.D.
dissertation, The Bialystok Branch of Warsaw University,
Bialystok 1986

Lecture Notes in Computer Science